St. Louis Community
College

Library

5801 Wilson Avenue
St. Louis, Missouri 63110

JACK NICHOLSON

By the same author

CLINT EASTWOOD : ALL-AMERICAN ANTI-HERO
with Gary Herman

JANE FONDA : ALL-AMERICAN ANTI-HEROINE
with Gary Herman

CHARLES BRONSON

ROBERT REDFORD

THE DEVIL'S VIRTUOSOS: GERMAN GENERALS
AT WAR, 1941-1945

JACK NICHOLSON

A BIOGRAPHY BY

DAVID DOWNING

STEIN AND DAY/*Publishers*/New York

First published in the United States of America in 1984
Copyright © 1983, 1984 by David Downing
All rights reserved, Stein and Day, Incorporated
Printed in the United States of America
STEIN AND DAY/*Publishers*
Scarborough House
Briarcliff Manor, N.Y. 10510

Library of Congress Cataloging in Publication Data

Downing, David.
  Jack Nicholson: a biography.

  Filmography: p.
  Includes index.
  1. Nicholson, Jack. 2. Moving-picture actors and
actresses—United States—Biography. I. Title.
PN2287.N5D68   1984   791.43'028'0924 [B]   83-40363
ISBN 0-8128-2953-0

Contents

Illustrations

JACK NICHOLSON

1

MUD'S BOY

'A town that has to be seen to be disbelieved'
Walter Winchell on Hollywood

1937 WAS A bad year for the airship *Hindenberg,* which crashed, and aviatrix Amelia Earhart, who probably did likewise. It is not fondly remembered by the Chinese, who were invaded, or the inhabitants of Guernica, who were carpet-bombed by the born-again Luftwaffe. To judge from his novel *Nausea,* published that year, Jean-Paul Sartre was profoundly depressed. And on the other side of the old world Stalin was off on another genocidal spree, making ready for the coming war by wiping out most of his generals.

For Americans, happily removed by an ocean or two from most of the above, the year's events were more propitious. Certainly the Great Depression was far from filled – it would take the War to do that – but the New Deal was being dealt and the worst days seemed to be coming to an end. In California, as if to demonstrate confidence in the future, two great projects were completed: the Golden Gate Bridge and Walt Disney's first full-length cartoon, *Snow White and the Seven Dwarfs*. And though no one knew it at the time, Hollywood's future was being born that year. Robert Redford, Jane Fonda, Dustin Hoffman, Warren Beatty . . . and one more. On 22 April, in a small New Jersey coast town not twenty miles away from the spot where the *Hindenberg* would die, June Nicholson, age 17, gave birth to a son; he was named Jack. But young Jack was led to believe that his grandparents, John and Ethel May Nicholson, were his parents and that June was his sister. Jack didn't learn the truth until June died in 1975, and he still does not know who his real father was. This information about his parentage is as reported in Nancy Collins' March 1984 interview of Nicholson in *Rolling Stone*.

John Nicholson, a part-time sign-painter, part-time window-dresser and full-time alcoholic, was not exactly the model a boy would have chosen. He left the family home soon after Jack's birth, and though he reappeared at irregular intervals, sometimes taking his 'son' along on endless bar-crawls, his part in the boy's upbringing was virtually non-existent. The adult Jack has never publicly expressed any bitterness over his 'abandonment', and when speaking of John has always sounded sympathetic rather than angry, but the impact on his childhood development, both good and bad, must have been immense.

Fortunately, the 'will-power' lacked by his 'father' was the dominating characteristic of his 'mother'. After John's departure she set out to make use of her qualifications as a beautician, and lacking the money to rent premises set up a beauty parlour in one of the house bedrooms. She was obviously good at her job: the business thrived to the ex-

8

tent that the family was soon able to move to a bigger house.

So, as the war years passed, the young Jack was brought up by a working 'mother'; his 'sister'/mother, June; and his 'sister'/Aunt Lorraine, fourteen years his senior. Through the house flowed a non-stop procession of women en route to and from beautification. It was an instructive time. He discovered, or so he said forty years later, that 'the key to approaching women' was 'unbridled curiosity'. He also learnt another priceless art – how to make friends with them.

He was, apparently, an infuriatingly likeable (or likeably infuriating) child. He bestowed nicknames on everyone – 'Mud' for Ethel May, 'Rain' for Lorraine, 'Shorty' for her husband – threw spectacular tantrums, and then earnt forgiveness with a flash of an already dangerous smile. At Roosevelt Elementary School he was the life and soul of most escapades, generally liked and admired by his schoolmates.

His teachers were rather more ambivalent. On the one hand young Jack was one of their brightest pupils, scoring straight 'A's with embarrassing ease. On the other he was decidedly prone to 'deportment problems'. He was suspended three times, once for smoking, once for swearing, and once for what is nowadays known as vandalism. Another school's basketball team employed tactics which Jack found unacceptable, so he comprehensively sabotaged their new electric scoreboard by way of revenge. On another occasion trouble seems to have brought out the nascent actor within; relegated to the dunce position for some minor misdemeanour he proceeded to compound the offence by covering his face in chalk-dust, standing there for all the world like a French mime tragedian.

For one school concert he dressed up in red crepe

9

cape and bellboy hat to sing 'Managua, Nicaragua'. But there is no reason to suppose that he spent his schooldays waiting for a tilt at showbiz stardom; like most boys, his days revolved around avoiding school-work, talking and playing sports, and talking sex. The latter eventually evolved into dating, but his school-marks managed to remain respectable. By the spring of 1954 he was earnestly considering the offer of an engineering scholarship at the University of Delaware, trying to decide whether his hatred of school could be held in check for a few more years.

It was a decision easier to ponder than take, and where better to ponder it than Los Angeles, where 'sister' June now lived? Perhaps there he would find the necessary inspiration. Perhaps the decision would be taken for him.

★   ★   ★

The Korean War might not have helped Korea much, but it had done great things for Los Angeles, a city which always thrived when the arms industry was booming. The young Nicholson, arriving from the East, must have been impressed by the sheer prosperity of the place, its aura of dynamism and growth, a materialist's paradise set amidst the sun-drenched palms. This was where the dreams had been woven by the men and women whose footprints graced Sunset Boulevard. This was the real America. He decided to stay.

In Hollywood, as in America at large, change was in the air, but as yet only in the air. This was the Eisenhower decade, that peculiarly flat interregnum between one Asian war and another. The rebels were still waiting for their causes, decrying social conformism but offering no positive rallying points for their disaffection. It was not a time of social protest; rebellion was individualistic, a matter of taking to 'The Road' or of snickering behind a dog-eared copy of *Catcher in the Rye*. Notions like the mass levitation of the Pentagon were a generation away.

Writing had always been considered the traditional haven of the rebel individualist, and it's no surprise that the young Nicholson had aspirations in this direction. But Hollywood too was getting in on the act, and the dramatic successes of Brando and Dean –1954 was the year of *On The Waterfront* and *East of Eden* – offered a more spectacular future for the young rebel in movies. Perhaps acting was the path to follow.

Either way he had to get inside the dream factory, and here the problems were immense. The film industry was faring less well than the city economically, and Nicholson himself was finding staying solvent a full-time occupation. He worked in a toyshop, hustled pool, played the horses, all in pursuit of his honourable crust. There was no time left for becoming famous.

Six months passed and he was about to give up, to return East a reluctant nobody, when good fortune struck. He landed a job in the MGM mail department, handling the daily avalanche of Tom and Jerry fan letters. It wasn't much but it was a start, an 'entry-point', and it provided him with the time and money needed to begin acting lessons and solicit auditions. One of the MGM producers actually gave him one of the latter, but Nicholson didn't learn his lines well enough. Another potential mentor told him wonderingly, 'Gee, Jack, I don't really know what we could use you for, but when we do need you, we'll really need you.'

He did secure a place in a local theatre workshop

called the Players' Ring, and this gave him the chance to begin learning his craft in earnest. He also enlisted in the beginners' class run by actor Jeff Corey, and there he met fellow-students James Coburn and Sally Kellerman, and two men who were to prove of great significance to his future career, Roger Corman and Robert Towne. He shared a flat with the last-named, and between them they went out in pursuit of glamorous actresses. Without success, however – according to Towne these lissome legends were not interested in 'nobodies'.

It was a good time nevertheless. Nicholson later told *Playboy* that it was a period of 'freshness and discovery of what acting was all about, of meeting new people and being inspired by other people's work, of watching an actor or actress who could hardly talk come into a class and then six months later suddenly do a brilliant scene.' It was also a period of high-spirited extra–curricular activity, of parties and surreptitious joints and gallon upon gallon of cheap red wine.

The service had to be fitted in, and Nicholson spent it as a fireman with an airfield-crash crew. 'In my asbestos suit I used to walk into the flames,' he said later. 'It gave me the most wonderful "high", this feeling of being other-worldly, of existing in another element.' But back in acting class he was still not providing enough 'highs' for Jeff Corey, who demanded some 'poetry'. The young actor, though, was not short on confidence. 'Maybe, Jeff,' he replied, 'you don't see the poetry I'm showing you.'

He knew he could do it, even if the rest of the world seemed depressingly loth to recognize his **poetry**. He needed another breakthrough. Chances

12

there were for others: Michael Landon was whisked away from one Players' Ring production to stardom in the television series *Bonanza*. It was possible, even in such times of shrinking studio payrolls. All Nicholson needed was a little luck, or perhaps a cinematic sugar-daddy.

2

THE LITTLE SHOP OF CORMAN

'Another De Laurentiis project, The Bible in the Beginning *(1966), was advertised as a fifteen-hour feature to be directed by nine men . . . Robert Bresson, invited to find an Eve for his 'Garden of Eden', brought back test footage of six potential stars, all of whom, to De Laurentiis' horror, were Negro or Indian . . . appealing to the Vatican for a ruling, he was told that Eve should be white, blonde and blue-eyed.'*
John Baxter, *Hollywood in the Sixties*

YOUNG HOPEFULS HAD been hanging around Hollywood since the building of the studios, but their chances had never been thinner. The American economy, boosted by the burgeoning automobile and petro-chemical industries, was booming as never before, but the film industry was for once ahead of its time, plunging with the railroads into a profound recession.

Ten years earlier, in Hollywood's post-war heyday, no one had bothered with such questions as 'Why do people go to movies?', but as the midpoint of the

14

fifties passed, the striking slump in audiences certainly started people asking the question, 'Why don't they go to movies anymore?' The answer was not difficult to find. The public was now being spoiled for choice when it came to leisure activities, and the movies were no longer *the* way of spending a relaxing evening. In particular, television had arrived. It cost less, there was no need to go out in the rain, it was new. For the movies to survive they had to offer something which TV could not. This might seen obvious in retrospect, but it was to be a lesson long in the learning.

For the time being the movie companies were thinking more in terms of cutting costs than of raising the standard of their product. The sprawling sets began to shrink as chunks of prime development land were sold off, fewer films were made, old ones were sold in lots to television, the number of actors under contract to the major studios was drastically cut back. The young Clint Eastwood, for example, was cast loose by Universal in 1956. Like many others he would have to make the big breakthrough elsewhere – in TV, Europe or, in his case, both – before Hollywood would welcome him back with a smile and a check.

But there was a third way through this world of shrinking opportunities, and it bore the name Roger Corman. Nicholson had initially met him at Corey's acting classes, and Corman must have found something to remember in the young actor, for in 1957 he asked him to take the lead in one of his quickie melodramas, *Cry Baby Killer*. It was to be the beginning of a long association, and one moreover which was uniquely suited to the preparation of Nicholson the future star. Corman, more than anyone else then working in Hollywood, was a film-maker who looked forward rather than backward. In many ways his methods were the methods of the future American cinema.

He had been making independent films since 1954, as producer, director, writer or any combination of the three. Then only twenty-eight, he soon earned a reputation as someone who got films made quickly, efficiently, stylishly and, most important of all for such times, cheaply. In the next thirteen years he was to make no less than forty-five movies, many of which have since been hailed as minor classics.

His methods were simple, innovative and profoundly influential. While the giant studios deployed their giant crews on giant sets, seeking giant profits from their giant markets, Corman used small crews for extensive location shooting. If he had to build sets, then he used them for as many movies as he could squeeze out of them. The smallness of the profit margin per movie was compensated for by the sheer volume of movies being made.

Flexibility was one keyword, and this carried right through the movie-making process, from production and direction through to the writing and performing of the frequently skeletal scripts. Professionalism was another, because such flexibility involved a great deal of skill, and Corman here was fortunate to have the services of such professionals as cameraman Floyd Crosby, scriptwriter Charles Griffiths and art director Daniel Haller. It took real talent to improvise at the sort of speed which Corman usually demanded.

Between 1954 and 1956 he specialized in making mass-market 'B' movies, mostly Westerns, gangster and sci-fi/horror films. But after this initial burst of mostly routine popcorn fodder, the films began to show increasing signs of subtlety. The genres stayed much the same, but the mood was more playful, as Corman began sending up the genres themselves with an endearing irony. Sexual role reversals were one consistent feature – the all-girl gang in *Teenage Doll*, the female sheriff in *Gunslinger* – and the gangster as a repellent victim was another, most notably showcased in *Machine Gun Kelly*, one of Charles Bronson's earliest successes. In most of the films, which to judge from the posters were overflowing with blood and gore, it turned out that emotional realities proved more decisive than mere physical action.

This was all the more noticeable when compared with the current TV output. Here the more traditional Hollywood verities were being regurgitated; problems were there to be solved through a judicious application of saintliness and the willingness to kill in self-defence. In Corman's films the solutions were rarely so clear-cut; for all of their outlandish appearance his movies were slices of their protagonists' lives, not the beginning, middle and end of their fight with fate. Consciously or not, Corman was moving into one of the vast territories where television had not yet staked its claim, the one marked 'neo-realism'. In a very different way Sergio Leone was to conquer the same territory with his spaghetti westerns in the sixties. The movies might be escapist, but they were far from dumb.

There was, of course, one good reason why television had not bothered to explore this territory. As any T S Eliot aficionado would know, there was no mass market for reality, neo or not. But there was a growing, and as yet largely ignored, specialist market – the nation's youth. John F Kennedy, Bob Dylan, the Beatles, the sixties, were only a few years away, and soon the likes of Brando and Dean, of the Beat Poets and the folkies, would be the norm rather than the exception. A version of reality, acceptably presented, would soon be a boom industry, and the 'youth market' would become the largest of those specialist markets growing up in the space where the old mass market used to be. For people like Nicholson and the many other one-day-to-be-famous names involved with Corman during this period – Francis Coppola, Monte Hellman, Dennis Hopper, Bob Rafelson – there could hardly have been a better way to spend an apprenticeship.

The way in which Corman made films could not but both broaden and deepen the knowledge of all those who worked on them. As Robert Towne succinctly put it: 'Roger would let anybody do anything no matter how bad you did it.' This wasn't just pedagogical zeal on Corman's part. The trust placed in improvisation, the flexible shooting style, the skeletal scripts, they all placed great responsibilities on those working on the set. If anyone had a good idea then in it went. If an actor felt like helping with the script, or the writer felt like playing a small part or helping out with the lighting then, provided he was competent, he did. On Corman's sets people found out about the art of making films whether they wanted to or not.

★   ★   ★

For Nicholson this 'learning period' with Corman was to absorb the better part of a decade, and it must often have felt like a long and frustrating wait for a breakthrough that would probably never come. He later said that he thought 'being discouraged worked positively for me', but being discouraged must also have been pretty depressing.

18

Cry Baby Killer was certainly not the sort of film to provide anyone with instant stardom. Teenager Jimmy Walker (Nicholson) is beaten up by three other teenagers when he tries to revive his relationship with ex-girlfriend Carole, but is not sufficiently deterred. When threatened with another beating he picks up a gun dropped by one of his adversaries and shoots two of them. Thinking he's killed them, Jimmy takes refuge in a handy storeroom with three handy hostages, a black employee and a terrified woman-with-baby. Police, crowd and hot-dog salesmen gather, his parents try and persuade him to surrender, but the baying of the silent majority outside only increases Jimmy's panic and he threatens to shoot his hostages if any attempt is made to storm his sanctuary. The police are about to lob in the tear-gas when Carole – remember Carole? – persuades Jimmy to see reason (and plead self-defense).

The film was made in ten days, cost only $7,000, and was shot virtually on a single set. The plot was hardly novel, and the whole exercise was reminiscent of the basic model for such 'man-on-the-edge' movies, Sol Siegel's tale of a potential ledge-jumper, *Fourteen Hours* (1951). But *Cry Baby Killer* had something. *Films and Filming* magazine, though finding 'the production values almost non–existent, the acting makeshift', noted the 'concise and unpretentious' story and 'the strongly humane attitude' on display. This Corman-in-a-nutshell appraisal was echoed by other reviewers, notably the *Monthly Film Bulletin* scribe, who found 'evidence of a direct honesty of approach lacking in the recent cycle of teenage exploitation vehicles'. The acting was euphemistically described as 'inexpert'.

Perhaps this was why Nicholson didn't make

another film for almost three years. Instead it was back to the acting classes, the red wine, and sporadic appearances on television. In the *Divorce Court* series he was almost a regular, and thoroughly enjoying himself. 'I was a great newspaper reporter . . . I used to improvise the lines and make up my own scenes in the background. They asked me back every week.' But bigger parts were harder to find, and Nicholson put his difficulties down to his face: 'I had problems because there's some overview of what people are supposed to look like when they're casting a film. I wasn't really anywhere. Neither grotesque enough to be a weird guy that took a lot of pills and stabbed people, nor good-looking enough to be the James Dean copy.'

As the decade ended things began to look up: in 1960, four films would be released with his name among the credits. *Little Shop of Horrors* was directed by Corman himself, and thoroughly typical of the films he was putting together around this time. Seymour Krelboind – all Corman films are full of such names – is developing a hybrid plant in the florists where he works, only to find that its favorite food is people. Seymour, a well-meaning lad, doesn't know how he's going to feed it, but fate comes to his rescue. First he accidentally knocks a man under a train, then accidentally kills a sadistic dentist. His boss accidentally kills an armed thief. All disappear into the voracious plant, which only pauses to belch out the thief's gun. Meanwhile two policemen – called, inevitably, Frank Stoolie and Joe Fink – are hot on the trail, and Seymour eventually makes the great sacrifice, offering himself, complete with hidden knife, to his creation.

Nicholson's role was small but memorable. He

played one of the dentist's patients, and a very peculiar one at that. When the dentist invites him into the surgery he croons 'oh goodie'. In the chair his enthusiasm grows; he thinks 'there's a real feeling of growth, of progress, when that old drill goes in'. The dentist, in a last desperate attempt to scare his patient, growls 'this is going to hurt you more than it hurts me', but all this elicits is 'oh goodie goodie, here it comes'. When the drilling stops the first time, the patient screams, 'oh my god, don't stop now', and when the dentist has finally made swiss cheese of his mouth he petulantly asks, 'Aren't you going to pull any?' Finally, speaking with a newborn lisp, he departs with the line, 'I can truly say I've never enjoyed myself so much.'

This beautiful cameo was only one of several in the film; others included a delightful hypochondriac and the imperturbable Fink and Stoolie. The plant was classically unconvincing. It's hard to argue with the reviewer who thought it 'the best full-length horror comedy ever made in two days'.

Nicholson's other three parts that year were larger but much less memorable. *Too Soon To Love* was the first of three films – all of them less than distinguished – which he was to make with director Richard Rush, with Jennifer West and Richard Evans as the young lovers caught up in an everyday story of unwanted pregnancy. It was standard fifties fare; the father was *really* to blame . . . after all, if he hadn't kicked up such a fuss in the first place then they wouldn't have had to hide their love in dark corners and . . . still, they're a sensible pair, unlike the society around them, and they really are too young to marry, so they have to get an abortion but there's no money so . . . but it all ends on a simperingly happy note. *Film Daily* found it 'an earnest probing drama of teenagers . . . treated with candor and dramatic effectiveness'. It might prove a 'sleeper', they thought. It didn't. Nicholson, as the young man's buddy called Buddy, could well afford to forget this one.

Studs Lonigan was a different matter. This was no 'quickie' thrown together to fill out a double bill, but a well-intentioned attempt to cinematise a well-known and reasonably respectable piece of literature, James T Farrell's trilogy of the same name. Unfortunately for all concerned, this story of a young man's trials and tribulations in the Chicago of the inter-war years was not very amenable to cinematic treatment. Like many such 'epic' books, *Studs Lonigan* derived most of its power and charm from the cumulative resonance of a narrative which sprawled all over the place, into and out of a large number of people's lives over a long period of time. The film, by reducing all this to a mere plot, only served to demonstrate how unimportant the plot was.

The director, Irving Lerner, had been involved in epics before – he had been supervising editor and second unit director on Kubrick's *Spartacus* – and he was aware of the difficulties he faced, noting that 'any one of the Farrell trilogy would be a challenge'. But, hampered by lack of money, lack of time, and a lack of talent in his leading actors, he failed to pull off the necessary miracle.

Nicholson apparently landed a part because he was the only applicant who'd read the three books. He played Weary, a member of the gang which battles for Studs' soul in competition with the 'nice girl', job and priest which he gets pregnant, rejects and eventually listens to (in that order). Reviewers picked out the gang scenes as the most realistic in the movie, but overall *Studs Lonigan* was rejected as a well-meaning failure.

The Wild Ride wasn't even well-meaning. Nicholson was back in 'B' movie territory and back in the leading role, this time playing Johnny Varron, a cry baby killer with a motorbike and less compunction about killing his fellow citizens. It was the sort of film which no one minded coming into halfway through, and it did nothing for his career. As he said himself, 'Before *Easy Rider*, if I was offered a part, the chances were that I took it. That was the reality of my situation.'

*   *   *

The next film was better, if only marginally so. A Corman 'B' western directed by John Bushelman, *The Broken Land* was a typical product of this period, both traditionally structured and chock-full of 'meaningful' statements in the contemporary style. Its plot could have graced, if that is the word, any of the TV western series then being shot behind every rentable piece of sagebrush. Nicholson played one of an ill-assorted group unjustly imprisoned by the over-zealous marshal-with-a-past. A waitress who happens to know about said past breaks them out of jail, whereupon the marshal sets out in pursuit. Eventually he recaptures them, killing his nicer deputy in the process, only to have the waitress spill the beans to the assembled townsfolk. Exit marshal, hissing and snarling.

The first line uttered by Nicholson's Will Broicous – another Corman name par excellence – was 'yeah, it sure is a lousy atmosphere', but generally speaking

23

his comments were even more philosophically pointed. 'I call it blood hunger,' he says of the marshal. 'It eats away at a man's guts, and it don't matter what side of the law he's on.' More tendentiously still, he reminds his fellow fugitive, 'It's not love that holds us together Dunston, it's hate. Hate for Kogan (the marshal) and for all the others like him in all the towns we've ever been in.' Yes, such lines really were written. The memory of them must bring Nicholson out in a cold sweat even today.

When he's not philosophising, Broicous tends to mock, and in this film the first hints of a future persona become visible. Lines like 'I'd take my hat off to you if it wasn't already off' may not be particularly sparkling, but it is possible to imagine the later Nicholson, from *Five Easy Pieces* or *Chinatown*, pulling them out with a slow drawl and a malicious twinkle in his eyes. And if this glimmer of light at the end of a long tunnel made *The Broken Land* a minor turning-point in his career, the year 1962 also saw a significant change in his private life with his marriage to actress Sandra Knight. For a few years at least the actor would lead a more settled existence, and it is perhaps no coincidence that those years were to see a broadening and deepening of both his commitment to, and his knowledge of, film-making.

His next two movies, both Corman Poe 'adaptations', were to play an important part in his development. Though neither offered Nicholson much in the way of an acting challenge, the first was to prove such a success and the second such a challenge in other ways, that both were to prove of lasting benefit to his career.

The Raven was directed by Corman himself from a script by sci-fi novelist Richard Matheson, well-known for his *I Am Legend* and *The Incredible Shrinking Man*. It was a 'tale of mystery and imagination' all right, but both these elements definitely took second place to the rich vein of humor which flowed through the film. The sets were magnificently Gothic, and Floyd Crosby's colour photography did them ample justice. The cast, which included the massed anarchic talents of Vincent Price, Boris Karloff and Peter Lorre, did ample justice to the script. Nicholson, who played the Zeppo character to this bunch of weirdos, must have enjoyed watching them ham it up. He got the girl in the end of course, not that anybody gave a damn.

The story began with sixteenth-century magician, Dr Craven (Price), visited by an irritable raven which turns out to be the metamorphosed form of another magician, Dr Bedlo (Lorre). Craven is obsessed with the disappearance of his wife, whom he believes to be dead, and he asks the raven whether he'll ever see her again. 'How the hell should I know,' the raven replies. 'What am I? A fortune-teller?' So the film's tone is firmly established.

Bedlo has been turned into a raven by evil magician Dr Scarabus (Karloff) for daring to challenge his supremacy in the magic arts. Craven turns him back into human form, meanwhile learning that a woman resembling his wife has been seen at Scarabus' castle. The two good magicians join forces and head towards the evil lair, accompanied by Bedlo's son (Nicholson) and Craven's daughter (Olive Sturgess). This, of course, is what Scarabus has been planning all along.

Craven's wife is indeed shacked up with the evil magician, but out of choice. No sooner have the good guys discovered this unpalatable fact than they are

25

dumped in a dungeon and told that Craven's daughter will be tortured unless he agrees to divulge his magic secrets. Unfortunately for the powers of darkness, Scarabus can't resist turning Bedlo into a raven again, and the bird proceeds to cut their bonds and so make possible the fantastic duel of magic which seals Scarabus' fate. The sixteenth century is made safe once more.

As far as Nicholson's career was concerned, the important thing was that shooting was finished ahead of schedule, leaving Corman with a few days paid-up rent on the Gothic sets. Hence *The Terror*. According to Corman, 'What happened was that all the interiors were shot in two days on the sound stage that had been used for *The Raven*. I didn't even have a script as a matter of fact.' According to Boris Karloff: 'I begged him not to do it. "You haven't got a story," I said. "That's all right," he replied. "I know exactly what I'm going to do . . ."' What he really wanted to do was shoot the sets of *The Raven*, which were still standing, and which were so magnificent. As they were being pulled down around our eyes, so Roger was dashing around with me and a camera two steps ahead of the wreckers.'

The story was made up as they went along, and it seems likely that Nicholson, who was playing the leading role, had as large a say in it as anybody. He was a Napoleonic officer, lost somewhere in the foggy marshes of a Hollywood Prussia, who is saved from drowning in white ice by a beautiful young girl (played by wife Sandra). She disappears, but the officer is brought back to health by a weird old woman, finding out in the process that the beauty can be found in the nearby castle of eccentric recluse Baron von Leppe (Karloff). He doesn't find her there at first, only a picture of the Baron's dead wife which looks remarkably like her. It turns out that the old woman is a witch bent on revenge for the Baron's murder of her son, and that the beauty is a somewhat insubstantial piece of flesh designed to drive the Baron to suicide. When the latter does go over the top and tries to drown himself by flooding his cellars, the officer saves the girl only to have her fall to pieces, literally, in his arms. Creep, creep.

Corman, as noted, directed the interiors, but he didn't have the money to shoot the rest of the film according to union rules, and since he personally was signed to the union, other directors had to be found. He later stated that 'at one time half the young film-makers in Hollywood did odd pieces on *The Terror*. Francis Coppola directed part of it, Monte Hellman directed part of it, Jack Hill, Dennis Jacob, Jack Nicholson directed himself when we ran out of directors . . .'

This was what made the film so important for Nicholson. He acted, he wrote, he directed. It was something of a cathartic experience, awakening in him an interest in film-making which went way beyond acting. From *The Terror* onwards he would rarely be involved in merely fulfilling one part of other people's visions; he would be sharing the visions, putting forward his own. And this of course could only benefit his career as an actor. He would be more able to shape his own roles, to built up an acting persona, to put across a more consistent image of his own making.

There was still a long way to go, but the next project was an interesting departure, marking his first credit as a screenwriter. He and friend Don Devlin had been invited to write a contemporary thriller for

27

Corman's group, and they rattled one off in three weeks. It was set in the Caribbean, which was much on the American mind at this time, and it centered on an assassination attempt, which soon would be. *Thunder Island* went before the cameras early in 1963.

The central character, played by Gene Nelson, was a professional hit man hired by a Latin American syndicate to knock off their ex-dictator in his pampered exile. An innocent family gets drawn into the plot when the killer selects the father – an ex-advertising executive now running, Bogart-style, a charter fishing boat – as his marine chauffeur. He refuses to take the job, whereupon the nasties kidnap his wife. He changes his mind. But the hit man turns out to be a miss man and the rest of the movie becomes an elongated chase, with the enraged father hotly pursuing his wife and her abductors.

The only real problem with the script was the scot-free escape of the dictator, but perhaps this is a 1980s prejudice. There was certainly a lot of political moralising in the air, and it was this that brought down the wrath of one reviewer, who considered that such questions were treated in 'a rather too glib and juvenile manner'. This, in retrospect, seems rather unfair; you don't expect searching analyses of contemporary problems in sixty-five minute 'B' movies. The same reviewer did admit that for a second feature, *Thunder Island* was 'decidedly above average'.

If only *Ensign Pulver*, Nicholson's next acting assignment, had been so glib, so juvenile. Directed by Joshua Logan with a lack of style which did ample justice to the script, this sequel to the successful Fonda-Cagney-Lemmon vehicle, *Mr Roberts*, would prove a low-point in more careers than Nicholson's. His role was mercifully small and uncredited, just

28

one of the hapless crew on the hapless boat in the hapless movie.

They say the darkest hour comes just before the dawn. Nicholson's own Hollywood daybreak, *Easy Rider*, was still five years away, but he was not to sink so low again. Since *Cry Baby Killer* he had made ten films, and there would be a further ten in those five years, but his position in the industry would slowly improve in their making. He would act in nine of them, write four of them, and play a significant role in the production and direction of several. In 1964 he was just a fairly unsuccessful actor with a few ideas, one 'B' movie script and a few scenes of directing behind him. By 1969 he would know what it took to make movies.

3

WHO WAS THAT
MASKED EXISTENTIALIST?

*'I like the western. I think the western is the closest
thing to classical theatres, for America, that exists.'*
Jack Nicholson, 1976

MONTE HELLMAN WAS born in New York in 1932, and
soon after that his family moved to California. He
eventually graduated from Stanford University in
Speech and Drama, moving on to do post-graduate
courses in cinema at the UCLA film school. He
worked in the theatre for several years, and it was his
directing of the first ever West Coast production of
Waiting for Godot which brought him to the attention
of Roger Corman. The 'King of "Z" movies' had one
he wanted directing, so Hellman made his film debut
with the auspiciously titled *Beast from Haunted Cave*,

and for the next few years did second unit and art direction work on a string of Corman movies, *The Terror* amongst them. In the process he met and befriended Jack Nicholson, who proved a kindred spirit when it came to ideas for making movies.

The two collaborated on a screenplay titled *Epitaph*, which according to Hellman was 'a semi-autobiographical thing about life on the fringes of Hollywood, a young actor knocking about, with a story about a couple of guys in which a guy tries to raise money to get his girl an abortion. It would have been the first of the abortion movies . . . that was still a taboo subject.' Corman provisionally offered to back the project, but different work intervened for the two authors. Hellman was to direct two movies in the Philippines, one for television and one for the cinema, both for Lippert Productions, the last of the major 'B' movie-makers. Nicholson was to write the TV one (from a Hellman–Fred Roos story) and play prominent roles in both.

Flight to Fury, the TV vehicle, did not prove a memorable film. Nicholson played a psychopathic killer in pursuit of illicit diamonds, wandering homicidally through the Far East like a premature B-52. He crashes his plane in a jungle, the gang fall out (with each other) with the usual threats and sneers, and no one gets any richer. Surprisingly, Nicholson later remembered the character with some enthusiasm: 'A tremendous psychopath. That's one of the early movies of mine that I do like. It's the one where I kill myself. The last line the guy says in the movie is "Joe, nobody can kill me!" and then he kills himself!'

Back Door to Hell wasn't much better, but it was more interesting. Nicholson played one of three American soldiers dropped into the Philippines just before the American recapture in 1944. Their job is to report back the location of enemy units, and to this end they enlist the help of some rather reluctant guerrillas (well, would you want to be recaptured by the US army?). The Japanese hear of their presence, and true to Hollywood form threaten to kill all the children in a particular village unless the Americans surrender. They of course decide to attack the village and . . . etc etc.

In other words a routine war movie. The problem with *Back Door to Hell* was the obvious level of intelligence behind the camera – Hellman and Nicholson were obviously trying to make something more than a routine war movie. And as a result the usual farcical heroics, which work in routine vehicles *because* they're farcical, seemed completely out of place amidst all the anti-war moralizing and an apparent attempt to use the jungle as a metaphor for something more profound than monkey-nuts. The two men were quite capable of making profound films, as the next two would amply show; their mistake here was to imagine that the flimsy 'B' movie structure they were working in could bear the weight of any serious intent. The film ended up dissipated by its own contradictions; the script was so bad the direction seemed overblown.

Back in America, Corman had had the time to reconsider the financing of *Epitaph*. 'He was afraid it was too downbeat,' Hellman said later. 'At that time there was a prejudice that you could make that kind of movie in Europe but not in America. But he said that if we wanted to make something commercial he would finance that. So we said "What's commercial?", and he said, "Well, a western's commercial." So we said "OK".' But being Corman, there was more. 'Then he said, "Well, if you're going to make one western, you might as well make two."' Of course. Who in their right mind would go all the way to Utah and make only one?

Hellman continues: 'So we rented an office and decided that Jack would write one and we would get someone else to write another. Several friends submitted ideas. Adrien Joyce (the pen-name of Carol Eastman) submitted a script which wasn't producible but was very interesting, and I had faith in her talent so we decided to go with her.'

Meanwhile Nicholson had already got down to work, and his intentions were not exactly what their backer had in mind. 'Roger wanted some good tomahawk numbers with plenty of ketchup, but Monte and I were into these two films on another level . . . We thought of *Ride in the Whirlwind* as a kind of translation of *The Myth of Sisyphus,* the Camus essay where man's only dignity is in his return down the mountain after pushing up the stone. That's what our film was about: three guys back from a cattle drive getting mixed up in some fracas.'

Carol Eastman had picked Jack London for her inspiration. In one of his stories a man looks at a picture of a gunfight which is hanging over a bar, and comments that life's just like the picture – you have no idea what led up to that moment and no idea what happened afterwards. This prompts his companion to recount an experience he once had. One day a woman had hired him to take her across the snows, never telling him of their ultimate destination, just pointing the way forward. Eventually they had caught up with a man on a sledge, and the woman had simply shot the man, paid off her driver and disappeared. He had never found out why she had shot him or what happened to her. This was the genesis of *The Shooting*.

In both films the verbal script was to be tailored to the intended mood. Nicholson in particular was delving into diaries from the period in question, and writing dialogue which reflected the semi-archaic modes of speech which he found there. The primitive level at which these people communicated, he felt, both reinforced and reflected the sense of man's isolation which the films sought to portray.

With the two scripts ready enough for shooting to begin, Hellman and Nicholson incorporated themselves as Proteus Films, accepted the necessary cheque from Corman, and headed out for the Utah Desert. They had a crew of only twelve, including two wranglers for looking after the horses. The equipment was equally rudimentary, consisting only of two reflectors, two cameras, one utility truck and a station wagon which had known better days. Neither truck could be used off the roads so the filming equipment had to be lugged everywhere on horseback. To complicate matters still further the terrain was none too solid, and the obvious foot- and hoof-marks left behind after each take meant that no two takes could be done in the same place.

But spirits were high. The two men were doing what they wanted to do, and what was even better, didn't feel responsible to anyone or anything for what transpired. As Hellman put it: 'I don't think we really thought that anybody would ever see the films. We thought they would be a couple more Roger Corman movies that would play on the second half of a double-bill somewhere. So any thoughts about doing something different were for our own personal satisfaction . . .'

*　　*　　*

34

In 1965 the western, to most people in America and Britain, meant *Rawhide, Bronco, Cheyenne* and other TV series, plus the occasional John Wayne offering at the cinema (it was *The Sons of Katie Elder* that year). All were firmly rooted in the old traditions of Hollywood's West. Narratives were explicable, heroes were clear-cut and clean-cut, morality was in and sex was out. For stories which revolved around violent conflict the violence itself was as chaste as the heroines. No one bled in profusion. In short, the genre had become fossilized. Ninety-nine per cent of westerns were as predictable as John Wayne's politics.

1965, however, was also one of the great watershed years of the post-war world, ushering in, along with the bombing of North Vietnam, a short period of remarkable political, social and cultural flux. Movies were not of course exempt, and westerns in particular were to provide a series of brilliant reflections on the state of American society and the wisdom of its latest Asian spree. In the period 1965–70 some of the best movies in the genre's history were to be produced, most notably *Hombre, The Wild Bunch, Tell Them Willie Boy Is Here, Hour of the Gun, Little Big Man* and Leone's first four westerns, culminating in *Once Upon A Time In The West.*

Several common threads ran through these disparate films: a souring view of frontier mythology, a corresponding reappraisal of the treatment meted out to the native American and the Mexican, and a redefining of heroism and its moral content in the western context. All could be seen in part as a reaction to America's current troubles at home and abroad; they were definitely films of the times, and in that sense new and challenging.

But in another sense they merely represented an

35

updating of the usual western morality play. The goodies might now be baddies and vice versa but the basic Hollywood tradition of narrative structure was not being tampered with. In each of the nine films mentioned, the audience came out of the theater with a good idea of what had happened and why. This, though predictable enough, was far from an unmixed blessing. As the Swiss director Alain Tanner was to say some years later: 'All the traditional narrative techniques brought to near perfection by Hollywood form the appearance of reality by the destruction of real space and time within a sequence or scene by fast-paced and quick cutting. This prevents the spectator from having a real view of space or time, and this is directly related to the ideological use of film in which the audience is led by the nose like a sleepwalker from the first scene to the last . . .'

These traditional narrative techniques were what was missing from *Ride in the Whirlwind* and *The Shooting*. As Nicholson himself said: 'What separated them from other westerns was the level of reality.' They were as uncompromising as the two men could make them.

The Nicholson-written *Ride in the Whirlwind* begins with three cowhands encountering a group of outlaws in the middle of nowhere, and being invited to share their hospitality. Unfortunately a group of vigilantes arrives, surrounds the camp and sets about smoking out its inhabitants. Two of the cowhands (Nicholson and Cameron Mitchell) manage to escape the trap, and seek refuge with a family of homesteaders. The latter have obviously never seen a Hollywood western, because there's no neat log cabin, no apple pie, no precocious kids and hardly a smile to be seen. Instead there's an existence verging on the primitive, an uphill struggle for survival given poignant expression in the recurring, Sisyphean image of the father hacking away at an obstinate tree-stump. The Bible, though frequently consulted, seems more like a Caucasian totem pole than a source of moral judgement. Morality is simply irrelevant in these circumstances, and its absence precludes any conventional notion of heroism. Survival is the only possible yardstick of 'success'.

The two cowhands are betrayed, and though they manage to escape once more, one of them is mortally wounded. So the film ends without resolution. Fate has dealt its cards, the karmic wheel has had a spin or two. The tree-stump remains. Or, as Bob Dylan put it in a song released the year before, 'life and life only'.

The Shooting has no homestead, nothing but a destination which nobody knows. Former bounty hunter Willet Gashade (Warren Oates) arrives back at the mine he works with brother Coigne, Leland Drum and the simple-minded Coley (Will Hutchins) to find Coigne gone, Drum dead and Coley incoherent. He eventually deduces from Coley's ramblings that Coigne has gone on the run after riding down a man and child in the nearby town, and that Drum has been shot by person or persons unknown.

A woman appears on foot, asks to buy a horse and offers Gashade money to escort her across the desert. She doesn't offer any explanations, and Coley becomes increasingly obsessed with her as their journey progresses, finally taking her life in his hands. This prompts the appearance of another rider, whom Gashade has for some time suspected was following them. His name is Billy Spear (Nicholson), a hired killer, and he clearly knows more of what's going on that Gashade (or, for that matter, the audience). He takes Gashade's gun, and when the woman's horse drops dead he leaves Coley stranded in the desert.

Coley eventually catches them up – he's found a dead man's live horse – but Spear shoots him, whereupon Gashade jumps the hired killer and smashes his gun-hand. Meanwhile the woman has disappeared up a canyon, having apparently sighted her quarry. Gashade runs after her, she takes aim, several shots ring out, and both fall to the ground with Gashade calling out the name 'Coigne'. The End. We leave *The Shooting* not knowing who has been shot by whom, let alone why.

In some ways the two films bore a remarkable resemblance to the new 'spaghetti westerns' coming out of Italy. The desert landscape, usually relegated in the traditional western to the status of an irritating impediment to easy travel – the *third* waterhole is always OK – becomes the dominating reality, dwarfing the humans who seek to cross it. The few signs of human habitation set within this wasteland seem wholly alien, fundamentally precarious. This land is not some vast expanse waiting submissively to be tamed by Adam's descendants, it's a killer, a bleacher of bones and a waster of flesh.

Its effect on the living is measured in close-up, the eyes three-quarter closed, the weary look, the exhausted sighs of the modern-day Sisyphus who knows that the mountain gets the last laugh. The leading characters of the Hellman-Nicholson films bear one, and only one, striking resemblance to Leone's *The Man With No Name*. The audience never finds out more about them than they actually see. The past is not filled in with apparently stray gossip and helpful innuendo. They are what they seem, no more.

The basic difference is more crucial. Leone's hero stands above the land; he has learnt to mould his life around it, to use it for his own ends, and this gives him both the traditional facets of heroic control and the opportunity to indulge his winning sense of humour. For the protagonists of *The Shooting* and *Ride in the Whirlwind* there is no such control and no possibility of real humor. They are pawns and they know it.

Pawns never win. They don't even make exciting moves very often. The problem with these two films, as Hellman and Nicholson were soon to discover, was that audiences liked exciting moves, liked the ease afforded by the traditional Hollywood structure. The story goes that an audience, viewing one of Antonioni's early films, burst into collective mirth when the camera followed one character down a long corridor. So used to seeing the middle of such an exercise cut out in the interests of swift narrative flow, they could only assume that the director was demonstrating his incompetence by leaving it in. *The Shooting* and *Ride in the Whirlwind* were to receive, in America at least, a similar reaction. Why is nothing happening? – that was the standard response from the few people who saw them. When's the action going to start? Who are we rooting for? What the hell is this film about? Movies with no beginning and no end ran counter to expectations in 1965, and to a large extent they still do in the mid-1980s.

Corman, shown the finished products, instantly realized their lack of commercial potential. The distributors agreed, and no one could be found to pay the asking price for the US rights. There were two other options: in America they could cut their losses and sell the films off to TV, in Europe they could try promoting them as art, via the festival circuit.

★ ★ ★

It was Nicholson who took the films to Europe, and the experience must have done his confidence no end of good. The audience at Cannes was rather more receptive than its American drive-in equivalent – for one thing it was watching the screen – and the two westerns provoked a great deal of positive interest. One of those present was Jean-Luc Godard, then in his heyday as a measuring-stick of cinematic innovation, and he liked them. Nicholson was naturally pleased. 'The fact that he liked the films very well really helped me in a lot of areas. In other words, his signature opened a lot of doors just because he doesn't really endorse anything that he doesn't really like.'

Reflecting on his European odyssey in 1972, Nicholson said: 'I was seven years younger then, and you know, I was very vibrantly into film, its ideas and its theories, and I hadn't even accumulated a lot of knowledge. I mean, I thought I had, but I hadn't. So their (European film-makers') conversations were very interesting to me. You know, and the beauty of it with these guys, if you really have something valid to say they're equally interested. They're available. This was when I first began doing anything other than acting. Here, whenever I would be talking to a director I would always have that feeling that either I was looking for a job or he thought I was looking for a job. I never really overcame that. And I didn't have that feeling in Europe when I was talking to these guys. I guess it's not done that way there.'

But despite the interest shown in Europe, the two westerns were still some way from gaining a wide release. The company that secured the French rights spent the next twelve months going bankrupt, and it was not until 1967 that the films were successfully launched in the capital. The critics were complimentary, and Nicholson and Hellman must have felt a warm glow of satisfaction. They certainly didn't receive much else; their total earnings from the two films were, according to Nicholson, a princely $1,400 each.

In America they had been sold to TV in the absence of any other offer, but were still to be shown when Hellman bought back the rights. *The Shooting* has been shown quite frequently at club cinemas over the last fifteen years, *Ride in the Whirlwind* rather less often. Time is still catching up with them, at least insofar as Britain and America are concerned.

From Nicholson's point of view they hadn't turned him into a household name, but they had increased his status within the industry as someone with something to offer, as far more than just another dumb Hollywood hopeful. He was proud of the films, and with good reason. For the first time he'd made movies which were, in part at least, a reflection of his own personality. His views had informed them, his talents had shaped them. He'd made his mark. A mark, moreover, which one of the most respected figures in world cinema, had pronounced interesting. He was getting somewhere.

4

FROM ANGELS TO MONKEES

'The bottom's full of nice people.
Only cream and bastards rise.'
Paul Newman, as Lew Harper, in *The Moving*
Target

IN THE YEARS 1965–8 the United States passed through a
social and political upheaval unparalleled in its
post-war history, with the 'establishment' under attack
from three distinct sections of its 'electorate': the racial
minorities, the Vietnamese, and middle-class youth.
These three struggles, though intertwined in the con-
sciousness of the time, were clearly separate. The anti-
war and civil rights movements were designed to correct an imbalance, to heal the obvious rift between rhet-
oric and reality; the 'youth revolt' was about something

42

else entirely. It was, for all its naivety, a revolt against the misuse of affluence; its thrust was individualistic, idealistic rather than materialistic, its concerns were emotional rather than political in the usual sense of the word. It found expression in the birth of a new sub-culture, centered around rock music and drugs, and imbued with a whole range of personal and political attitudes which ran counter to those prevailing in the society as a whole.

Needless to say, a new sub-culture implied a new market, and in the ensuing decade the 'youth revolt' would prove a commercial bonanza for the very people it derided. Fifteen years later the contradictions are plain enough. But in 1966 this was not the case. In 1966 it felt like a real struggle, and for people like Nicholson, living in Los Angeles, the battles were raging on the doorsteps. The black riots in Watts, the youth riots on Sunset Strip in late 1966 and early 1967, all seemed like the birth-pangs of a new and uncertain age.

And the new lifestyle, for those who could afford it, seemed so full of self-righteous sense. Why not expand your mind with drugs, soft or hallucinogenic? Why restrict yourself to one sexual partner when all the world was love? Why not let it all hang out? Across California, in these years, you could hear the egos bursting out.

The film community, which always liked to imagine itself in the vanguard of changing tastes, was more affected than most. Nicholson, radically-inclined in any case, was more at home in this new world than his marriage, which reportedly expired, amicably, when his and Sandra's life-priorities began to diverge. His career was influenced just as dramatically. The film industry, and particularly Corman, soon came alive to the enormous possibilities inherent in the 'youth revolution'.

43

Young people had less interest than ever in sitting at home watching television with their parents; they wanted their own entertainment, and if the cinema could provide it then something yet might be saved from the wreckage of the old mass market. Films about motorbikes, drugs, relationships, music. Six of Nicholson's next seven films would fall into this category. The last of them, *Easy Rider*, would lift him out of obscurity for good.

Hell's Angels on Wheels and *Rebel Rousers*, the two 'bike movies' made in 1966–7, were about as memorable as a takeaway hamburger. Full of hackneyed images, constructed around hackneyed plots, they sunk beneath the weight of the illusion that a pleasant sensation can somehow be construed as a meaningful lifestyle. If this was the youth revolution then society had got its wires crossed again.

Nicholson himself was not immune to self-deception in this matter, as he demonstrated when talking to *Rolling Stone* about one of the films. 'I've owned a couple of motorcycles,' he said. 'That feeling, that bike-riding feeling, I've had that, I know what that's all about. Actually, I was very lucky on my first motorcycle movie because it was the only one that has the actual Hell's Angels colours in it . . . And Sonny Barger – I met Sonny on the picture and spent some time with him. He's essentially an American-firster you know. The way he described his thing struck me as totally respectable, the American Way, man. The way to get it, he just wants to show that a small group of people can form their own society, based on their own morality, and not have to take shit from anyone.'

Hardly a definition of the compassionate society, but then a lot of Californians in the late sixties were expressing sentiments which now seem merely crass. In the same interview, given in 1971, Nicholson went out of his way to explain the 'happening' at Altamont – someone was stabbed to death by Hell's Angels for daring to touch a motorbike – in tones that seemed to justify the outcome. For someone who was to become the intellectuals' favorite film star it was a strange line to take.

The two films took his career nowhere; in both he had parts which, though prominent, were completely undemanding. Nor does he seem to have contributed anything other than his acting ability. After the self-fulfilling experience of the two westerns, such work must have seemed almost demeaning.

The next part was even smaller, but the film, *The St Valentine's Day Massacre* was in a different league to the 'bike movies'. Corman directed, but for once he had more than a shoestring for support: Twentieth Century-Fox had offered him the first big budget of his career. He made the most of it, creating one of the classic gangster movies.

The company didn't interfere too much, insisting only on a few minor changes at the editing stage. Corman did think, however, that the casting could have been better. He wanted 'a very distinguished cast . . . Orson Welles as Al Capone and Jason Robards as Bugs Moran.' The company agreed to Robards, 'but they said that Welles would never play Capone and that he was impossible to deal with . . . I later met Welles and he said he would have been delighted to play Al Capone. Also some of the supporting players were contract players whom I wasn't happy with.' Still, a cast list containing Robards, George Segal, Ralph Meeker, Jean Hale and Bruce Dern could hardly be called undistinguished.

Anyone expecting a gangster equivalent of crab monsters attacking Gothic castles was in for a shock. Instead of exploiting the sensational elements of the

45

story, Corman turned it into a quasi-documentary, giving rein to the more lurid side of his imagination only when the narrative demanded it. Certain such scenes stick in the mind, particularly the bloody assassination of one gangster in a florist's, amidst a sea of crimson-spattered wreaths, but overall the impression remains of a director firmly restraining himself in the interests of letting the events speak for themselves. Unlike its contemporary *Bonnie and Clyde*, an equally fine but totally dissimilar movie, *The St Valentine's Day Massacre* did not deal in romanticisation, in image-manipulation, did not attempt to share the gangsters' sense of their own importance. As Philip French noted in *Sight and Sound*, 'the totality of the image the film creates tends to suggest that crime is a part of the American system, a product rather than a perversion of it.' Another reviewer thought the film 'a cool, dispassionately logical narrative which makes complete sense of the intricate quarrel between Capone and Moran, and also portrays very graphically the way rackets were run as respectable big business whilst open warfare was waged on the streets.'

Nicholson, for unknown reasons, turned down the slightly larger Bruce Dern part in favor of playing a getaway driver. At this point in time his heart does not seem to have been in acting, and perhaps one line of dialogue was all he could summon up enthusiasm for. Nevertheless it was a beauty. As one gangster greases his revolver cartridges, another asks him what the hell he's doing it for. 'It's garlic,' Nicholson explains, 'the bullets don't kill ya, ya die of blood poisoning.'

*   *   *

During this period Nicholson seems to have been more involved in writing. He was currently engaged in finishing the screenplay for *The Trip*, a project which he had sound reasons for thinking would provide him with a more contemporary image than any on offer in secondrate 'bike movies', particularly if Corman allowed him the part he was writing for himself, that of the all-knowing acid guru.

He took acid himself as part of the necessary research. 'The psychiatrist blindfolded me for the first five hours. I regressed, re-experienced my own birth, was in the womb. It's hard to verbalise this kind of thing. I was an infant thinking I was wetting myself and talking with a small voice. I even felt I was going to die. The doctor said "Let yourself go." I did. I died. It was liberating. Then my wife came to get me. I mixed her up with my mother. And all the while I'm schizo and could look at myself. And was going with it. The old actor training. Go with it.'

But Corman wouldn't let him have the role. Bruce Dern got it instead, and according to him, Nicholson 'was pissed off because Roger wouldn't use him. He wrote the part for himself and Roger wouldn't use him.' Dern himself wasn't much happier at having to play second fiddle to Peter Fonda: 'I was fed up because Peter Fonda was a star and I wasn't. Peter couldn't act . . . All I knew was I had to carry this lame through a movie for thirty-five minutes and he went on to be a star the rest of the time.'

Certainly the whole film revolved around Fonda, the first-time tripper, and it must be said that his performance was hardly conducive to taking the story seriously. He played a director of TV ads, fed up with his wife, who decides to drop acid in search of a coherent life. It's arranged that he'll do so at the house of friend Max (Dennis Hopper), under the supervision of friend John (Dern). At first his visions are sweetly erotic, yo-yoing

47

him with loving ease from wife to girlfriend and back again. But then things start getting heavy, and he rushes out of the house and into a city full of Cormanesque medieval images. Scenes with a little girl at her house, in a disco, in a laundromat flow swiftly by. Eventually he gets back to Max's, only to find that John is out looking for him and that Max, fearing the police, won't let him stay. His girlfriend finds him in a cafe and the following morning, his mind and life suddenly coherent, he reveals the incredible truth – he loves her.

So much for Hollywood acid. As more than one reviewer gleefully pointed out, the acid visions bore a remarkable similarity to the TV ads which tripper Paul had been making. This was not wholly the film-makers' fault—acid trips are as hard to cinematize as they are to verbalize—and Corman's use of color was nothing if not vivid. But still the feeling persists that nothing new is being experienced, that what is on offer is merely a kaleidoscope of thoroughly predictable fantasies.

Corman also had trouble with the distributors. He himself had taken acid before making the movie, and was feeling unusually sanguine about humanity's prospects: 'I saw man in a loving universe and I tried to reflect that in the film. But AIP cut the film after I was finished to give it a negative look because they were worried about certain outcries against drugs.' Whether these cuts substantially damaged the film it's impossible to say.

The reviews were decidedly mixed. Judith Crist was appalled. 'The subject matter enables the director to make a totally incoherent movie with erratic, repetitious and fake-arty effects that simply nauseate, both intellectually and physically.' The British *Films and Filming* magazine did not review *The Trip* until 1971, and by then Nicholson was important enough to be included in the condemnation. 'It does give you a look into the heads of Corman and Nicholson,' the reviewer thought. 'The former is not unnaturally hung up on a lot of Hammer, American International, symbolic Poe, while Jack's five easy pieces all had big tits and hips. So if one of them is hung up on medieval sado-masochism and the other is high on sex, it doesn't leave much for Fonda and Hopper to do except punctuate every word with "man".' Significantly, Bruce Dern, in the role Nicholson had written for himself, was exempted from all criticism.

The upmarket *Sight and Sound* magazine thought differently. According to Phillip Strick the movie was 'constructed with a nice line in humor, a dazzling sense of composition, and the customary ear for formalistic dialogue which derives its unmistakable poetry from the total sincerity with which it is spoken.' Man. The *Monthly Film Bulletin* was similarly agog. *The Trip* was 'a brilliant piece of film-making', and in some scenes the 'terrifying abyss between reality and fantasy' had been made 'suddenly tangible'.

So much for critics. Watching *The Trip*, one is certainly made aware of the terrifying abyss which separates film-making from wishful thinking, and the holy misconceptions of the American youth revolution are more than once made suddenly tangible. As a waitress remarks in the film, with rather more pertinence than its makers seem to intend, 'What's the matter with you guys? Isn't the real world good enough for you?'

Apparently not, for Nicholson, Susan Strasberg, Bruce Dern and acid were all back together again within the year to make the Richard Rush-directed *Psych-Out*. Once again the cameras would zoom in and out of multi-colored inner landscapes, and once again the resulting film would prove less than compulsive.

49

Some things had changed though. In the year which separated the two movies a lot of bad scenes, to use the vernacular of the times, had gone down. The San Francisco dream had outlasted only a few of its casualties, the dealers had moved in on the accessory market, and all the other survivors had set up record companies. This souring was good news for the film industry; love and peace were terribly difficult to turn into melodrama, whereas disillusionment was a theme which Hollywood scriptwriters could write variations on in their sleep.

In *Psych-Out* Jennie (Susan Strasberg), a deaf seventeen-year-old, comes to San Francisco's infamous Haight-Ashbury district in search of her brother Steve (Bruce Dern). She's sheltered from a police raid by three members of a run-of-the-mill rock band: Stoney (Nicholson), Ben (Adam Roarke) and Elwood (Max Julien). Later, in an art gallery, she sees one of her brother's pictures and gets on his trail. Stoney takes her to see another group member, Dave (Dean Stockwell), who points them further on their way. They find her brother's flat but he's disappeared, and is now apparently on the run from some angry creditors. While Stoney continues the search Jenny falls prey to lecherous Dave, who's given her a dose of hallucinogens in order to lower her defenses. Unfortunately for him she learns that Steve's in trouble and rushes off hallucinating. Steve, meanwhile, has barricaded himself into his house, prior to setting it ablaze. Stoney and Dave eventually find Jenny tripping away among the cars on the Golden Gate Bridge (where else?) and Dave obliges the audience's sense of justice by getting himself run over.

Psych-Out was no better than its plot, which was a fairly weary turn of a rather blunt screw. The trip sequences were no better than average, the direction

50

generally uninspired. The music, supplied by second-rank groups like The Seeds and the Strawberry Alarm Clock, was not successfully integrated into the story and not particularly good in any case.

Nicholson himself was not entirely dissatisfied in retrospect. It was, he thought, 'a pretty accurate movie as far as exploitation movies go. For instance it was at the height of the love-flower movement, and what I liked about my character was that he kept saying, "enough of the bullshit, we're in it for the money".'

It was a sentiment which also summed up the film.

★   ★   ★

Although he was not to know so at the time, *Psych-Out* was to be the last of Nicholson's pre-stardom films as an actor, closing the curtain on a long and frustrating apprenticeship. For Roger Corman he had nothing but praise and gratitude. In 1975 someone suggested to him that Corman was 'one of the most vital forces in the American cinema', and Nicholson couldn't agree more. 'The guy's made eighty movies. Look at the directors who've worked through his system: Francis Coppola, Monte Hellman, myself, Irving Kirschner, Dennis Hopper, Bogdanovich . . . What directors have the major studios produced? You see right away that the guy's a superior person. He's the best producer I've ever met in the business. His taste is what it is. The man carried me for seven years. I feel tremendously indebted to him, but there's no emotional blackmail involved. *He* doesn't feel that I'm indebted to him. He's the only man in the movie business from whom, if he said "you got a deal", I'd write a cheque without seeing the movie. He's that honest.'

Nicholson had enjoyed himself: 'I worked a lot with

51

the same group of young actors and writers and we used to hang around the same coffee shops in Hollywood. It was fun. We were young. And anything could happen in that crazy Hollywood of the 1960s.'

He had learnt a great deal about movies and their making: 'The films I was doing were pretty much for a specific market. They weren't seen, and haven't been seen by many people. If they had, I may never have worked again. But a movie's a movie. You get the experience and start learning what registers about yourself, what you should and shouldn't do, and can and can't do. And while it's not tremendously ego-gratifying or financially rewarding, it's background. Once you've been really *bad* in a movie there's a certain kind of fearlessness that you develop.'

His opinion of the films themselves was to change as the years passed. In 1971 he could claim that 'even if I hadn't made them, I wouldn't resent spending ninety minutes seeing them, which is *not* true about a lot of movies I see.' Five years later he was less sanguine: 'I hate seeing my old movies now. I take no pleasure in them whatsoever.'

*　　*　　*

The Monkees' movie *Head*, which Nicholson co-wrote and briefly appeared in (as himself) marked both the end of his old career and the beginning of a new one. It was not a commercial success, it was not a film for which he or anybody else would be remembered. In its very nature, as a wittily self-conscious exploration of the Monkees' strange rise and fall, the film looked back rather than forward. But it did mark the beginning of Nicholson's long, intermittent professional relationships with director Bob Rafelson and producer Bert

52

Schneider, relationships which were to push him, as an actor, through the barrier of invisibility and out into the starry spotlight.

Bob Rafelson had begun his media career while doing military service in Japan, disc-jockeying for forces radio, translating Japanese films and advising the Shochiku company as to what movies they could hope to sell in the United States. His term of service over, he joined CBS in New York, working as a reader and story editor for David Susskind's prestigious 'Play of the Week' television series.

In the early sixties Rafelson moved across the continent to become an associate producer at Universal. Reportedly sacked after a violent scripting row—he is said to have overturned his boss's desk in a fit of anger— he joined forces with a fellow producer, Bert Schneider, and together they set up Raybert Productions. Rafelson then hit on the idea of turning the Dick Lester Beatle movies into a madcap television series. Two musicians and two actors were chosen to form the 'American Beatles', and the Monkees were born.

They were successful beyond all expectations, if with a rather younger audience than that the Beatles had attracted. They had a string of well-deserved hits – well-deserved in the sense that the songs were good, imaginative pop music – and the TV series stayed high in the ratings for a considerable length of time. A full-length feature film seemed a natural enough idea, though it seems that the parent company and Rafelson differed as to why. Columbia simply wanted to squeeze a little more revenue out of an already lucrative source, but as far as Rafelson was concerned 'Head was never thought of by me or my partner as a picture that would make money. What I felt was that we were entitled, since we had made for Columbia an enormous amount of money in their record division and in TV sales, to make a picture that would in a sense expose the project.'

While the movie was gestating in his mind Rafelson met Nicholson, and they hit it off immediately. They decided to co-produce and co-write the film, with Rafelson directing. Perhaps Nicholson was interested simply because he got on with his new friend 'Curly', perhaps he was hard up, and perhaps the project was sufficiently different to be challenging. His friends thought he'd lost his mind. 'What the fuck are you doing, working with the Monkees?' he remembers them saying. But he liked 'Curly'; 'I thought the guy was very honest, very open. He blew my mind a few times. I said, "Don't get me up at full creative amp – let's write a fair movie and do the best we can. Don't cop out on me, because I won't like it, I'll be very upset." And he never did. We made exactly the film we wanted to, an honest expression about a particular phenomenon: the suicide of the Monkees.'

The plot of *Head*, if such a random sequence of events can be called a plot, begins with the lovable American moppets arriving at a bridge-opening ceremony, whereupon Micky jumps overboard to dance an underwater ballet with some convenient mermaids . . . the four appear in concert complete with screaming fans, intercut with Vietnam War footage, and then suddenly (everything happens suddenly) find themselves in a war movie . . . back at the concert hall, dummy replicas of the group are being torn to pieces . . . then Micky finds himself on a TV show, no, sorry, in a desert with a coke machine that doesn't work . . . the Italian Army surrenders to him . . . the group are hired to play the dandruff in Victor Mature's hair for a commercial . . . finally, they are carried away in a large glass tank.

Written out like this it sounds thoroughly silly, a kind of psychedelic Marx Brothers without the gags. One reviewer thought *Head* 'the kind of movie I can imagine a man would make (and enjoy), if he had just seen the Ohio Express (a particularly innocuous pop group) on an afternoon teenybopper hop show, read a few issues of *Sixteen*, and then talked to the Monkees for a couple of minutes about the state of existence today.'

Paulene Kael, writing in the *New Yorker*, seems to have had more idea of what the movie-makers were getting at, but not much more sympathy. She found that the only novelty was in the selling, 'in convincing kids that they are visually sophisticated when they buy old jokes and blackout routines as mind-blowing, psychedelic, McLuhanite collages . . . This is the kind of material, taken from all over, that the Monkees have already worn out on TV, only much worse. The movie might have worked for bored kids at kiddie matinees, but the film-makers got ambitious. The by now standard stuff of girls squealing as pop idols perform is not even convincing when they're squealing for the Monkees, and when this is intercut with documentary footage of the suffering and horror of war, as if to comment on the shallowness of what the film-makers are manufacturing and packaging and desperately trying to sell, the doubling-up of greed and pretensions to depth is enough to make even a pinhead walk out . . .'

This was slightly unfair, if only because most of the greed was Columbia's and most of the pretensions Rafelson's and Nicholson's. Moreover, as if to defy such criticism from the word go, the latter had covered themselves by virtually inserting the same criticism within the script. In a sense it was exactly what the movie was about. The familiar theme tune had new words: the 'young generation with something to say' was now 'a manufactured package with no philosophies'. The group are described at one point as 'God's gift to eight year-olds', and Peter Tork philosophically observes that 'even manipulated experiences are received more or less directly by the mind'. Particularly when the manipulation is shown to be manipulation, as in the scene where Micky tells Rafelson 'Bob, I'm through with it', and stumps off through the painted backdrop.

Some reviewers found the film refreshingly honest. Richard Combs thought it 'the apotheosis of the late sixties psychedelia', a 'satire on the solipsism of image-making'. Teresa Grimes noted the film's 'exposure of the process of exploitation that any media product has to go through.' And there seems no doubt that those who made the film – Rafelson, Nicholson and the Monkees – were genuinely trying to say something about the phenomenon of the group's packaged success. According to Nicholson it was all the Monkees' doing: 'They're the ones who put out all that stuff about "our music is canned". Very honest cats. They took the chance that it would ruin them, and ultimately it did. They created their own negative image, really, and that's what the movie was all about. In fact, at a certain point, we finally did have a confrontation on this thing – with the Monkees – people were flipping out, Bert (Schneider) was yelling, Curly was yelling, but by that time the movie was all over.'

5

AMERICAN ODYSSEYS

'There is no more new frontier
We have got to make it here . . .'
from *The Last Resort* by Don Henley and
Glenn Frey

Head, according to Rafelson, 'made no money, coming out some time after the Monkees' popularity had
begun to wane; hardly anyone saw it, and those who
did were mostly mystified by it.' But it had given him
an insight into his co-writer's talent: 'Jack had abandoned his career as an actor at this point,' but while
they were writing the movie, he 'would act out all the
parts, as would I, and my eyes were just glued to the
expressions on his face and the intensity he brought
to the performance in a script conference. I told him
that the next time I made a picture he had to be in it.'

Meantime, two other long-term acquaintances of Nicholson, Peter Fonda and Dennis Hopper, had been developing the idea of an expensive bike movie, and together with Terry Southern (the future author of *The Magic Christian* and *Candy*) had written a plot outline. They took it to Corman, who was interested in the idea, but Sam Arkoff, the President of American International, had no faith in Hopper's ability to bring the project in on time or within the budget. He turned it down.

Fonda and Hopper's next port of call was BBS – the new Rafelson/Schneider/Steve Blauner production company – and the first person they saw there was Nicholson. 'Hey read this, we want to make a movie,' they said, shoving the eight-page outline into his hands. He took them up to see Rafelson and Schneider, and the latter was either very impressed or feeling very adventurous. He wrote out a personal check for $650,000. *Easy Rider* was away and rolling.

Nicholson was not personally involved at this stage, but when reports of on-location difficulties began filtering back to the BBS offices from New Orleans, it was decided that someone ought to be keeping a fatherly eye on the two riders and their budget. Nicholson was dispatched, nominally as an associate producer, but more as a general adviser. He introduced Hopper to some experienced colleagues, cinematographer Laszlo Kovacs and production manager Paul Lewis.

The part of George Hanson, the alcoholic young southern lawyer, had been earmarked for Rip Torn, but he dropped out of the film for reasons that remain obscure. There were some reports of a major row between him and Hopper, but others implied that Torn had simply dropped out. The actor later denied this, and Nicholson later admitted that he didn't know the truth of the matter. 'But,' he added, 'it sure didn't do me any harm playing it.'

That must rank as one of the great understatements of cinematic history. *Easy Rider* was to be one of the few films that could legitimately be said to have changed the course of that history, and to prove the old adage that being in the right place at the right time more than compensated for the quality of what was done there and then.

The film's storyline was simple enough. Two young men, Fonda's Wyatt – also known as Captain America – and Hopper's hairier, moustachioed Billy, make enough money out of a cocaine deal to finance a dream trip to the New Orleans Mardi Gras on their shiny Harley-Davidsons. Riding east they encounter a cross-section of American civilization: a hitchhiker, idealistic but struggling communards, a farmer and his family, and a lot of small-town bigots. In one town they are thrown into jail for being generally undesirable, and are only saved from violent depilation by the intervention of a young, cynical, and somewhat sozzled lawyer, George Hanson. He decides to accompany them, partly for the hell of it, partly because there's a brothel in New Orleans which he's heard wonderful things about. They initiate him into the joys of dope, but later the same night the bigots sneak up and kick him to death in his sleeping-bag. Wyatt and Billy carry on eastward, arriving in New Orleans to enjoy the Mardi Gras and sample the delights of the famed brothel. This turns, in more ways than one, into a bad trip. Back on the open road an exultantly stoned Billy announces, 'We made it, didn't we?' Wyatt, albeit dimly, knows better: 'We blew it.' Soon after this laconic exchange, a redneck trucker tries to scare Billy with his shotgun and kills him instead. He then shoots Fonda to cover the traces. The film ends on the image of burning motorcycles.

The storyline is one part of the film's story. The music used was mostly first-rate, and employed to stunning effect against the majestic scenes of the American wilderness through which the two young renegades ride their chrome steeds. And the narrative structure was, in any case, precisely that, merely an elongated hook on which to hang a succession of cameo scenes, each designed to dramatize an American problem or solution circa 1969. These scenes were neither cinema verité nor subtle; they were simply there to make points, to tot up the odds against the heroes or anyone else making it through. And, despite lapses – the crassness of some dialogue and images, Fonda's wooden acting – the points were made with an admirable clarity.

In many ways *Easy Rider* was made as a modern western: the settings, the names and the notion of new frontiers all fitted neatly into the traditional canon. But it was a peculiar western, an inside-out western perhaps. These heroes were travelling east, away from those fields of paradise which had lured the nineteenth-century pioneers. Nature does not threaten them, the towns are not experienced as havens from the awesome elements, the savage natives, the threat of starvation. Now it was all the other way around: the elements, seen through a dope-raised awareness, seemed mysterious and benign, whereas the towns, and their savage natives, posed the mortal threat. Civilization, once the goal, was now the enemy.

Billy and Wyatt are not angels of course; their

dream, like the original American dream, has been paid for in the misery of others, by all the casualties which their drug deal will carry in its wake. Nor are they particularly bright, a point brought home by the supposedly more intelligent Wyatt when he congratulates the careworn farmer for 'doing his own thing in his own time.' But no matter how guilty, how involved they are in the social mess which eventually kills them, in one respect the pair are naive enough to be virtual innocents – they know, intuitively, that they and their society have lost something vital. They don't know what it is, but they and the audience sense it, in the natural beauty of the landscapes, in the pathetic commune, in the mindless aggression of the 'civilized'. They never do find out, a fact which Wyatt realizes — 'we blew it' — even if Billy doesn't. Travelling, in the end, is an avoidance, not an answer.

George Hanson is both more truly innocent and more intelligently worldly. He is, despite the brevity of his appearance, *Easy Rider's* central character. He's 'trapped America, killing himself' Hopper explained. He's the well-meaning liberal, driven to drink, a man liable to ramble on about the Venusians under the influence of his third joint. He's cynically aware enough to advise his clients that he can get them off, provided they haven't killed anybody, 'least nobody white'. And he's deeply puzzled as to how such a state of affairs could have come into being. 'This used to be a helluva good country,' he slurs, 'I don't know what happened to it . . . People talk about freedom, but when they see a really free individual it scares them.' George Hanson is clearly a character with a future, if not in this film then certainly in others. There is something quintessentially contemporary about him, something that transcends the fashion-ableness of Harley-Davidsons, drugs and rock music.

Nicholson's performance won him rave reviews. 'A wonderful actor named Jack Nicholson is magnificent,' trumpeted Rex Reed; 'a brilliantly witty performance,' wrote Tom Milne. In the *New York Times* Vincent Canby said: 'As played by Jack Nicholson, George Hanson is a marvellously realized character.' None of which, needless to say, would have mattered a damn if the film itself hadn't proved such an overwhelming success, bringing in receipts in excess of $35 million. *Easy Rider* had touched the legendary pulse of the times. It had, as Paul Warshow wrote, expressed 'a "mythic truth", and although a minority of Americans have had the feeling for years, it has never before been given such clear or moving expression in a piece of mass entertainment.'

What was this 'mythic truth'? That there were bigots in Texas? That the old American myths were no more than that? Only partly. What *Easy Rider* caught was a turning-point in American history; its plot read like a summary of the nation's experience over the previous decade, the dream, the attempts to practise what was preached, the banging of young heads against the walls of an establishment which waged war on an Asian people and held its own subject minorities in a modern form of serfdom. And the outcome? Nixon elected, the escalation of the war, the sacrificing of the 'Great Society' to pay for that escalation, the cutting down of those like Luther King, Malcolm X and Bobby Kennedy who dared to dissent. Billy and Wyatt might be small fry, but almost despite themselves they end up on the wrong side of history. The trucker is more in tune with the society than they are. It is the audience's awareness

62

of this dismal reality which makes the closing scene of *Easy Rider* one of the cinema's most potent evocations of social despair. The dream is over, with a vengeance.

*   *   *

Easy Rider was one of the first major commercial films to give expression to that sense of failure which, in its many and varied ways, was to dominate the seventies. To understand the mainstream cinema of that decade, and Nicholson's starring role within it, it is neccessary to comprehend, however sketchily, just what that failure had been.

This is obviously not the place for an in-depth analysis of capitalism, socialism or, for that matter, seventh-day adventism. Suffice it to say that during the years 1945–68 most of the world had experienced a period of unprecedented economic growth. Indeed, the youth market which sprang into prominence in the western industrialized world during the sixties was very much an offshoot of that growth. But hand-in-hand with material prosperity there had grown a dissatisfaction with the uses to which it was put and with the political powers which decided those uses. This phenomenon was not confined to the West; parallel movements were occuring in the industrialized East, if with a rather different emphasis.

The late sixties saw the political expression of this dissatisfaction reach a high point: the polarization of American society on the issues of Vietnam and civil rights, the 1968 'uprising' in France, the 'Prague Spring', the Cultural Revolution of China, were all prominent evidence of 'high tide'. From 1969 the waters were clearly ebbing, with establishments everywhere reconsolidating their positions.

In terms of powers, that is. The hopes of the sixties could not be forgotten as easily as they were suppressed, either by communards in New Mexico or dissidents in Bratislava. The establishments had not recovered their moral authority, merely reasserted their physical and legal strength, leaving large sections of their communities with the enduring feeling that something in the state of proverbial Denmark was exceedingly rotten.

Mainstream cinema could not but reflect this situation, particularly in view of the fact that the majority of its audience was now drawn from precisely that section of the society most suffused with an awareness of its recent history. The new stars would be chosen democratically, as film stars always are, on the strength of their ability to reflect social reality. They could not be establishment figures in the traditional way because the establishment was morally bankrupt; they could not be liberal crusaders in the traditional way because the crusade had already been lost. It was exactly these two certainties – the old values, the possibility of real change – which had perished in the late sixties. The new stars had to reflect new certainties, or perhaps variations on uncertainty.

Here a distinction has to be drawn between period and modern movies. A period film, whether set in the past, future or, like *Star Wars,* both, could still deal happily in moral absolutes. Situations could be set up in a realistic enough manner to make individual heroism both morally justifiable and practically potent. A world without telephones or swift transport, for example, is a world in which one man or

64

woman can dominate a community, for good or ill. A similar effect can be contrived by juggling with futuristic technology. As long as all powers can be concentrated in the hands of Darth Vader, the Jedi can hope to return in triumph.

But modern-dress movies mean taking account of the limitations imposed by the world their audiences experience. And the dominating reality of that world has become the power of the state. The new hero was automatically cast as an anti-state figure in moral terms, and, since the state was to all intents and purposes impregnable, a loser in political terms.

There were ways around this. The most popular has been the setting up of situations in which the hero-individual can call on both his own potency and the power of the state to defeat adversaries located both within and without the establishment hierarchy. *Dirty Harry* and *Death Wish* are two classic examples of how such movies are constructed, Clint Eastwood and Charles Bronson the two most prominent examples of actors who have found superstardom through playing such roles. Their characters, in these and many other movies, are essentially establishment renegades, identifying the social problems they seek to eliminate as a function of the state's lack of moral backbone. As such, both films and characters carried a grain of truth, made all the more dangerous, in the opinion of many, by the mountain of grains they choose to ignore. Like monetarists, these heroes juggle effects in a bid to obscure causes. Their answer to the sense of failure was, and is, a grasp for the past.

The truly new hero, on the other hand, knew that the past could only be re-lived in movies. His negative mission was to reflect the uncertainty and desperation, both within himself and the society at large; his positive mission was to re-sow the seeds of anarchy left lying around by the iconoclasm of the sixties. He was an ordinary individual, living in the presence of the absence of the hopes raised by the last decade. He had to represent a blend of success and failure, an awareness that the latter was implicit in the former in modern America. Since the state was all-powerful, he had to recognize that the political and personal realms could not be brought together successfully. The political realm was barred to him, beyond his reach, so success could only be defined in personal terms, in successful relationships, sporting triumphs, in localised victories against an arm of the system, in a purely impotent but nevertheless satisfying awareness of what was really going on.

Nicholson, more than any other actor in the seventies, was to bring this truly new hero to fruition.

* * *

But first, a slight hiccup. While *Easy Rider* was still in the works Nicholson landed a part in the Minnelli-directed, Streisand-starring musical *On A Clear Day You Can See Forever*. Well, even the best angler sometimes lands an old boot. Two things had attracted him to the deal; the amount of money and the chance to sing. 'I was fascinated by the idea of someone who doesn't sing doing a song. I didn't want to talk or whisper it, and they promised me that they wouldn't dub it.'

They didn't. They simply left it on the cutting-room floor. Unfortunately they didn't leave the rest of the film in the same place. Streisand did her now familiar act, with rather less manic surety than usual,

Yves Montand was occasionally given room to look suave, and Nicholson seemed . . . out of place. His part was cut to such an extent that his presence in the film was largely inexplicable, and what little sense could be made of his character was none too convincing. The actor got an early inkling of all this when, arriving on set to play a rich hippie, he was told to get his hair cut. 'That was the key to the whole thing and I realised there and then what kind of time it was going to be.'

★   ★   ★

After completing *Head* Bob Rafelson had done some writing; three partial scripts to be exact, all centering around the same character but not connected in any other way. Uncertain of where to go from there, he had taken the bits to Carol Eastman, Nicholson's long-time friend and the writer of *The Shooting*. The three of them had several discussions, and it was agreed that Eastman would develop the character as a composite of Nicholson and her brother, utilising scenes which the two men had gone through in real life. While she set to work on the screenplay, Rafelson went out scouting locations.

Five Easy Pieces opens with Bobby Dupea (Nicholson) living the working life in southern California, moving from manual job to manual job, drinking hard and playing hard among the bars and bowling alleys. He has the sort of girlfriend half of him needs, a pretty, empty chatterer who doesn't give him time or reason to think.

But Rayette (Karen Black) also threatens to tie him down, and this is a fate which he can't accept. Bobby needs to keep moving, needs to keep having fun.

Even a traffic jam is experienced as a personal prison, until he finds a way to make it fun. This is no personal quirk; on the contrary it expresses the fragility of his connection to the world he inhabits. For Bobby, as the audience soon learns, is an escapee from another world entirely, a family of eminent musicians living a semi-hermetic life in the northwest.

Things are bad enough when the fun stops and starts, but eventually it grinds to an ignominious halt. His friend Elton is dragged away by the police, he learns that Rayette is pregnant and hoping to marry him, and last but not least he hears from his sister that his father is dangerously ill and that he is expected to return home.

He doesn't know what to do with Rayette. When she asks him whether he loves her, he can only reply, 'What do you think?' He can't say yes because it isn't true in the way that she means it to be true, in terms of marriage and commitment. He can't say no because he does care for her, or at least feels responsible for her. It's the same with his family. He doesn't want to return home, but he feels obliged to. He's stuck, and that's the one thing he can't afford to be. Together they head north.

En route they pick up two lady hitch-hikers, one of whom is volubly obsessed with all the 'filth' and 'crap' choking the modern world. They're going to Alaska where it's 'cleaner'. Bobby knows better though. That was 'before the big thaw!' he tells them. Stopping at a roadside diner he has trouble ordering what he wants, because it doesn't happen to be one of the precise combinations on the menu. He wittily defeats the waitress in the ensuing argument, but doesn't get his order. Back in the car the 'filth-obsessive' is full of admiration for his skill in 'beating the system'. Again he knows better: 'But I didn't, did I?'

He dumps Rayette in a nearby motel and reaches 'home'. Here his directness and apparently free spirit attract his brother's 'fiancee', but only temporarily. 'Where would it lead?' she asks. 'A man with no love for himself, no respect for himself, no love for friends, family, work, *anything* – how can he ask love from somebody else?' He knows it too. As he tells his stroke-incapacitated father: 'I move around a lot, not because I'm looking for anything, but to get away from things that go bad if I stay.'

He must move on again, regain the freedom that makes his life bearable. Abandoning Rayette, he hitches a lift in a truck bound for the far north, even though he knows that 'the big thaw' has already come.

The critics were mostly congratulatory. Stephen Farber found the film 'remarkable for its scepticism and understated complexity . . . remarkable for the perception and precision with which it delineates an individual character.' Anthony Macklin thought it made 'most American movies look fake', *Film and Filming* thought it a 'key work in the American cinema's recent appraisal of a morally decaying society, in which people are unfortunately only connecting with themselves.' The *Monthly Film Bulletin* reviewer found 'the complex character of Bobby Dupea unusually real.'

The paying public liked it too. Loved it even. For Nicholson it was the breakthrough he needed, the full realisation of the star potential he had shown in *Easy Rider*. From this point on he was a star.

★   ★   ★

69

Why was *Five Easy Pieces* such a success? Clearly because Bobby Dupea was an archetypal figure of the times, a man, as Nicholson himself said, who was vainly searching for some validity in his life. The actor understood the feeling: 'The search for me and for the character is compulsive. There's never been a time in my life when that wasn't going on. I suppose that's partly the coincidence of when I was born and where, plus whatever fantasies I have as a person. So naturally I feel the search is a way in itself. Looking for validity is not a detective story but a continuing thing.'

If George Hanson was this searcher in embryo, Bobby Dupea was clearly a functioning prototype. And if *Easy Rider* was a film about the closing of the open road, *Five Easy Pieces* was about a more despairing reality, the fact that the open road led nowhere. Bobby is not prevented from continuing his odyssey by rednecks, nor persecuted for wanting to be free, just channelled, as much by his own sense of responsibility as anything else, into emptiness. His life has become no more than a never-ending search for sensations, his style one of child-like obstinacy. The positive side to his character, which ensnares both the audience and Catherine at the start, is fully brought out. He relishes things, he enthuses, he bowls every ball at the bowling-alley as if it were the last. He's direct, he's clever, he cuts through the bullshit and the hypocrisy with a glee that is thoroughly infectious. He doesn't trust answers, and we the audience share his misgivings. Not only is he clever enough to triumph over the waitress in the famous diner scene, he's also wise enough to realise the pettiness of that triumph.

If the film had continued in this vein, working its

way comfortably towards a suitably mock-heroic end, it might be possible to agree with those critics who considered *Five Easy Pieces* just one more celebration of the freewheeling hero's struggle for self-expression in a stultifying society. Fortunately the film doesn't cop out like that, settling instead for increasing complexity, making it more and more difficult for the audience to find comfort in identification with the central character.

As the action proceeds the neon emptiness begins to shine more and more out of Bobby's eyes; he is clearly not a happy man. His iconoclasm seems to have no positive aspect, seems perilously close to nihilism. He's not being straight with Rayette, he can't be, and instead he merely treats her cruelly. When he re-enters the family womb it's equally apparent that he can't be straight with them. He can say outrageous things, display a form of honesty, but that particular form seems more and more akin to dishonesty. The film, which up to this point has largely empathized with Bobby's view of the world, now subtly shifts its allegiance, seeing him through the eyes of his family circle.

They are shown as living an over-sheltered life, as expressing themselves through constricted emotional channels, but it is also clear that they have worked out exactly that compromise with reality which Bobby cannot work out. Catherine rejects him precisely because she realizes that his 'liberation' has been gained only at the expense of his ability to sustain a real relationship. And deep down, he knows it too. When he breaks down in front of his father Bobby is expressing, in Rafelsons's words, 'an agony of displeasure over the life he was leading'. This is no hero in the traditional mold.

Bobby Dupea is a witty, attractive, knowing failure. All the simple solutions of the sixties have turned to dust in his hands. There's no need to shoot him off a metaphorical Harley-Davidson, because he's no threat to anyone but himself and his friends.

6

HOLLYWOOD SHUFFLE

'You've got to gamble. The movie industry isn't a slide rule business and never will be. It's still the world's biggest crap game.'

Richard Zanuck

WHILE *Five Easy Pieces* was doing business round the world, its star was passing his thirty-third birthday. He hadn't had an easy ride to stardom, except in the punning sense; he was the last of the 'class of 1937' to make the big breakthrough. But perhaps this was as much a blessing as a curse. He noticed that 'people have begun to treat me differently', but he felt able to 'control it'. 'You can make people treat you the way they always have, if you demand it,' he said in May 1971.

And he would so demand. Determination was

definitely one of Nicholson's prime character traits. His friend Harry Gittes – whose name would be hijacked for the role in *Chinatown* – noticed Nicholson buttonholing influential people after the *Easy Rider* success, 'introducing himself and making himself unforgettable, one person at a time'. The actor himself was quite willing to accept the need for self-promotion. 'There are two ways up the ladder,' he said, 'hand over hand or clawing and scratching. It's sure been tough on my nails.'

This apparent ruthlessness, in the Hollywood context, amounted to little more than an instinct for self-preservation, and Nicholson was also well-known for his easy-going nature and his loyalty to old friends. Most of his close companions at this time had been so for many years. Robert Towne and Sally Kellerman had been co-learners at Jeff Corey's acting classes, Carol Eastman he had known even longer.

The 'women in his life' tended to change with rather more frequency between the break-up of his marriage in 1967 and the beginning of his long relationship with Anjelica Huston in 1973. Model Mimi Machu, who appeared under the name of I J Jefferson in both *Psych-Out* and *Head*, and ex-Mama Michelle Phillips were the longest-lasting (or perhaps simply the most-publicized). Nicholson had a lot of 'anti-family feelings', and thought that 'a lot of the things that people are fucked up about at this moment can be traced back to family structures.' He was interested in a 'new kind of family', but saw his efforts in this direction as 'a lot of the reasons for my chaotic relationships'. His relationship with his ex-wife was cordial enough, and he saw his daughter Jennifer, now seven, frequently.

His lifestyle, according to the gossip columnists,

was marked by a heavy appetite for sex and drugs. He both agreed and disagreed. 'I've taken all the drugs, balled everybody, gone everywhere,' he is reported to have told *Newsweek*. 'I'd love to be able to say I've balled everybody, indulged in every kind of shit, gone everywhere, although I haven't,' he told *Rolling Stone*. His love of marijuana has never been disguised, and it was presumably hallucinogens he was referring to when admitting to 'giving up drugs' after finding himself and Dennis Hopper 'up a tree after spending the night on D H Lawrence's tomb'.

He was definitely a man of his generation, albeit a rather older member of it than most. In the late sixties he actually bought land for a commune in New Mexico, without ever living there himself. The inhabitants were driven out by armed locals after six months, then replaced by a new group of young settlers some time later. According to Nicholson in 1976, the land had eventually become a bandit haven. He seemed amused by the whole story.

Politics, for him as for most of the American 'movement' during this period, were 'just a part of living'. He was 'into influencing people subtly', he said in 1971. 'I won't go on any political bandwagons . . . I'm into affecting the society in which I live but not overtly, not by carrying placards telling people what to do. In the long run, I just feel that would limit my own sense of what is useful.'

The same attitude was brought to bear in his choice of films to admire and to make. He eschewed the direct political approach of Godard and other like-minded directors. Godard, Nicholson said, thought that 'to make an entertaining movie while Vietnamese are dying for what he considers to be piggish social reasons is to be a totally decadent artist. And he certainly is not going to be entertaining in the face of that. He's making movies now exclusively as essays.' Nicholson doubted that these 'essays' would achieve the desired effect. 'Who is it that he would have to change? . . As I say, I'm totally respectful of it, but I don't think it's accomplishing a lot . . . it's not propagandizing an audience . . . he's working in a very refined style . . . you don't make this kind of movie for a mass audience. Everybody makes movies and hopes everyone sees them and everyone likes them. And that they're helpful to everyone, entertaining to everyone, or something to everyone. But in essence – you know – movies have different styles. And he certainly is working for a more intellectual audience than average, and he doesn't give them newness. You know, they already either agree or disagree with him.'

Nicholson, in classic American style, thought politics more a matter of experience than of organization. Rohmer's *Claire's Knee* was one cinematic example he could empathize with. 'Ultimately, it was a political film. This isn't a theory or a locked-in political trip but I believe that film says one thing by implication: that a film can allow intelligent people to express themselves about complicated ideas . . . By showing these kinds of films, correlative thinking will become popular, or at least fashionable, simply because a popular, fashionable media is presenting it. It will make people react differently . . . correlative thinking is rare . . . people don't understand the relationship between their detergent and their befouled water.'

This was the sort of film he wanted to be involved with, and though such movies were some way from Godard's 'locked-in political trip', they were also some way from the traditional Hollywood narrative

76

film. Nicholson felt that 'by showing certain situations, by showing the way things are, you can effect change. I don't write story-movies.' He was, he admitted, intent on remaining within the commercial Hollywood mainstream, but he denied that this involved compromising with the establishment: 'I still do what I want to do.'

And at one level what he wanted to do was simplicity itself: 'Film-making. Just film-making. I don't have a big truth that I'm trying to tell. I just try and relate honestly, to see the truth and convey it about a given situation the best I can. As an actor, as a writer or director, I always have a sense of what the truth of a moment is while I'm working on it, and that's what I'm trying to communicate. The audience is there, they're in tune, they know what's coming down, and more and more complicated things are getting across.'

But there was a contradiction here, or at least a complication. Telling the truth was one thing, 'affecting the society I live in' quite another. As Bobby Dupea, he had just given a wonderful exhibition of the limits of 'honesty', of how not to 'affect society', at least in any positive sense. What was the way *forward*? Nicholson saw this as the central creative problem facing any film-maker with a social conscience. 'It seems that all we do is reflect and most of the reflections appear to be negative today. And how does the artist perform that other service in reflecting a positive, inspiring image? And still remain coherent and true to what you see – not what you think.' It was a question that would hover over all his films in the seventies, and there's little reason to suppose it will suddenly be answered in the eighties.

Of course, the very fact that Nicholson was asking

himself and the industry such questions made him an unusual star by the standards of the 'cultural boney-ard'. But it also made him a much-needed one. The industry, facing its gravest crisis as the new decade began, badly needed help in its bid to emulate and surpass the more thoughtful European approach to mainstream cinema. Nicholson, for his part, was well-placed to grasp the opportunities offered by an industry in the throes of transition. They could only benefit each other.

*   *   *

By the end of the sixties the major Hollywood studios had become a tawdry shadow of their former glittering selves. The great moguls had gone, the backlots had been turned into parking lots, the huge staffs were still shrinking. People were having their own dreams, often in public, not waiting breathlessly in cinema queues for a pre-packaged reverie. The city was covered in smog and the studios were immersed in gloom.

Or so it seemed to those sunk in nostalgia for the days of drunken, star-spangled glory. In fact, salvation was at hand; a new industry was fast gathering strength in the womb of the old. Four particular developments were bringing a gleam back into the eyes of the accountants.

The first was the swift growth of a new domestic market to take the place of the old mass market which television had stolen away. The new audience was predominantly young, with approximately seventy-five per cent of its members between the ages of twelve and thirty, a good proportion of them college graduates. This latter group exemplified the cinema's new status; it was becoming a prestige leisure activity, not simply an accepted way of spending two hours in an uncomfortable seat. People were more and more visiting their cinemas for a positive reason, because they wanted to see a particular film; the old, passive, 'entertain me for an evening' function had been taken away by television. This shift implied, potentially at least, a rise in film quality, but this was not what excited the studio accountants. They were more interested in the potential for higher prices. A positively committed audience would be prepared to pay more.

Easy Rider, which more than any other film had demonstrated the existence and extent of this new market, also played a prominent role in bringing the second new development to the studios' attention. It was obviously possible to make big money-spinners on a relative shoestring. There was no need to carry the enormous overheads of major studio production if independent companies could supply the product for the majors to distribute.

The third development offered more of the same. The immense success of the 'spaghetti westerns' far beyond the land of their birth (and, to a lesser extent, the success of the Far East-made Kung Fu movies) made evident the sudden growth of a genuinely global market. Hollywood would no longer be so reliant on domestic American sales.

Fourthly, the change in social mores which had characterized the previous decade offered the movies a chance to steal a march on television. Movies could be graded for exhibition to different age-groups, whereas television, esconced in the bosom of the family, had to have a 'U' certificate for everything. When it came to showing sex and violence in ever-more explicit detail, TV just could not compete.

As the impact of these developments began to be appreciated, the major studios began the necessary restructuring of their operations. Large chunks of their productive assets were either sold off or re-geared to production for television. Their hold was tightened on the domestic distribution channels, their worldwide operation expanded. Hollywood's famous companies might be losing their place as the world's premier source of movies, but they were firmly intent on remaining the fountainhead of movie-retailing.

The films themselves would be made by the new independents, which were sometimes truly independent and sometimes mere subsidiaries of the majors. They would bear the financial burden and take the consequent risks of production, but they would all be ultimately – that is to say, commercially – accountable to the major distributors. The new 'studio' became a meeting between the producer, director, writer and stars (all complete with agents) of a particular project.

In the long run this sundering of the financial and creative ends of the movie business was to have disastrous consequences in terms of film quality, but initially it seemed to the creative 'end' like a release, an escape from the land of the philistines. At last they were free of the meddling mogul syndrome.

One of the independent companies, actually a semi-independent subsidiary of Columbia, where this sense of artistic liberation was most marked was BBS. This was partly because the company had made a fortune out of *Easy Rider,* partly because many of the more talented graduates of Roger Corman's informal academy of movie-making were now gathered under its umbrella. It was in the BBS offices that

Nicholson could most often be found during working hours; elsewhere in the building Bert Schneider, Bob Rafelson, Dennis Hopper, Henry Jaglom, Laszlo Kovacs, Bruce Dern, Karen Black, Peter Bogdanovich and others could be discovered making deals, editing movies or simply shooting the breeze. On one wall of the reception room, neatly framed in chrome, were posters from the Paris of 1968.

All of these 'film people' were used to producing on a shoe-string, to the making of films in which ideas were as important as narrative structure. All of them had lived and breathed the California of the sixties, and their work now tended to reflect the turning inwards, away from the social sphere and into the realm of individual experience, which typified the period 1969–72, in rock music as much as in movies. It was a strange time for these men and women; the door of opportunity had opened up for them – here they were, suddenly the hottest property in town, the so-called 'Hollywood New Wave' – yet the world they were to portray, with the honesty that was their trademark, was one of closing options, of an America still torn by war and a crisis of self-confidence. And if in some ways they resembled the rock stars who lamented the state of the world from behind the massive shelter of their bank balances, it cannot be denied that they made some remarkably innovative films. Their output, as Stephen Farber noted at the time, both reflected and criticised 'contemporary experimentation in the area of personal relationships, the questioning of traditional conceptions of identity. Their interest in reassessing American myths . . . with tentativeness and compassion instead of anger, and their success in creating complex unheroic characters were welcome new qualities in American movies.'

In 1971, at places like the offices of BBS, it was not difficult to find people who were optimistic about the future of movies.

*   *   *

Jeremy Larner wrote the novel *Drive, He Said* in the early sixties, and it was brought to Nicholson then with a view to him playing the character of Gabriel. Nothing came of the project until eight years later when Nicholson, asked by BBS whether he had anything in mind for his directing debut, submitted the novel as one of several possibilities. Schneider and Rafelson liked it, and while *Head* was being made, the project was agreed in principle. The success of both BBS and Nicholson over the next two years solidified the deal.

Larner's book was a 'college novel', ahead of its time when written but far from distinctive in its setting by the time it came to be filmed. This presented Nicholson with his central problem. He liked the book, but he was not too happy with its milieu: 'Knowing already how many college films were going to be done and the point of view that was going to be taken in them, I was hesitant. I thought the material would by that time be a commercial drawback . . . I didn't really want to go into a film with things already going against me, because most things I have created other than as an actor have always had a certain lack of commerciality about them because of the point of view I take about things. Because I've had a certain amount of access to the tools of doing work I've always been fairly uncompromising just in terms of technique – I don't do much positive character development, I don't try and make it favorable to one market or one group or anything like that.'

But, commercial or not, he did want to make the film. 'I felt it was a subject through which I could say a lot I wanted to say. One of the things I like about the college film is that when people are naive and young, for me they have the licence to *state* a philosophy; it never plays right with older characters. If you're working with an academic community as a microcosm, it is more organically right that characters can speak dialogue with a more philosophical turn. The milieu does not make it overly pedantic, as it would be if you had two milkmen walking along talking about the poetics of playing baseball or the psycho-sexual dynamics of taking part in team sport.'

The credits on *Drive, He Said* read like a summary of Nicholson's career past and future. Jeremy Larner shared the screenwriting with the director; he had been promised a shout in the process from the beginning, he wanted to learn about film, and at BBS during this period no one was denied the chance to make their own mistakes. Steve Blauner co-produced; Bill Butler was the cinematographer, as he would be five years later on Nicholson's Oscar-winning *One Flew Over The Cuckoo's Nest*. The two leading roles, those of Hector and Gabriel, were filled by relative unknowns William Tepper and Michael Margotta, the former having been chosen by Nicholson because he found both character and actor equally irritating. For the rest of the cast it was a matter of bringing in old colleagues. Karen Black played Olive, Robert Towne her professor husband, Henry Jaglom another professor. Bruce Dern, offered a choice of two roles, opted for the basketball coach. He and Nicholson had been together in five of the latter's last eight films, and he found that the director's chair suited his old friend. 'Jack was really wonderful to work for in that he's just brilliant with actors . . . it was a pleasure to work for him.'

The film's storyline follows a few weeks in the life of two college room-mates, the Reichian-style revolutionary Gabriel and the Greek-majoring basketball star Hector. Their lives both interact and provide comment on each other. Hector is having an affair with Olive, a bored professor's wife, and having trouble living up to the demands of his monomaniacal basketball coach. As his problems with Olive increase, so his game suffers, and the coach's pressurising becomes more unbearable than ever. Meanwhile Gabriel and friends have interrupted one game for a 'guerrilla festival', and been carted off to jail for their presumption. Back at college he receives his draft notice and sets about making himself unfit enough for the medical board. He takes this too far for his own good, pushing himself into a dangerously real insanity. He tries to rape Olive, who has just found that Hector has VD and that she is pregnant by him. Escaping his pursuers, a naked Gabriel releases all the reptiles from the college biology laboratory . . .

The storyline, though dramatic enough, is less important than the characters. Larner had taken the title from the end of a Robert Creeley poem —

> drive, he sd, for
> christ's sake, look
> out where yr going

— and the film centres on the fact that each of its *dramatis personae* is so wrapped up in his or her own problems that they can't see where they're going. The key to finding out, according to Larner, Nicholson and Reich, lies in an ability to release one's own sexual power. Each of the film's characters is distanced from his or her sexuality – in the widest Reichian sense – in a different way. According to Nicholson, 'Olive is the freest of the characters. Gabriel goes crazy under the stress of his vision. Hector has difficulty in making the connection between his physical abilities and his place in society. Hector and Gabriel represent totally opposed philosophies, but they are living together, and neither is completely wrong or right, neither is meant to be wholly sympathetic.'

Shades of grey are not, of course, particularly popular with the punters, and many reviewers lamented the lack of a character with whom the audience – themselves – could wholeheartedly identify. They also found Gabriel too extreme, Olive too 'ill-defined', and the characters as a whole both mentally and physically 'unattractive'.

Nicholson had answers for all these criticisms. He knew that 'simplification' was good for 'audience connection' but he wanted complexity anyway. Gabriel was an extreme character from the beginning; he had to go right over the top or no one would realize that something serious was happening to him. As for 'ill-definition', Nicholson had no intention of giving his characters 'a limp leg, a puppy dog, a nice personality, just to get audience identification, because the fact that they are human beings is why I'm interested in them.' As he told another interviewer, it simply wasn't interesting or challenging to create characters 'that I already know are attractive to the audience right down the middle of main street.'

Above all he denied the 'ugliness' charge. It was a telling comment on some film critics, he felt, that they should object to a love scene on the grounds that the lovers were less than beautiful. Nor was he trying to make statements about the ugliness of society. *Drive, He Said* reflected 'the way that most people's relationships in life are at the moment.' Nowhere in the film was it suggested that this was part of the human condition; on the contrary, 'Every character in the film at some point speaks of their own inner sense of poetry, if nothing else, of their own desire to have a life beyond what they really are at the moment.'

But, and it was a big but even in the brief heyday of the 'New Hollywood', rebutting criticisms neither got the reviews rewritten nor made the film more commercial. *Drive, He Said* won praise in some quarters, but they weren't particularly influential quarters. Lil Picard of *Interview* magazine thought the film perfectly expressive of the times, that 'Jack Nicholson is an artist and proves it'. The *Monthly Film Bulletin* praised the 'deceptive casualness' with which the characters were 'shown to spill uncomfortable over the tidy confines of their chosen images', lauded the film for being 'neither sloganized nor brought to any specious resolution'. At the Cannes Film Festival the buffs were divided but earnestly so – fist-fighting broke out in the stalls between fans and foes.

The popular critics and the public, however, were less interested. The film was a dismal commercial failure. Nicholson, though naturally wishing that this had not been the case – it wouldn't help when it came to financing future projects – had no particular regrets. He thought it was 'a very good first film . . . I mean, when you're doing a first film, unless you're just somewhere else and you've never really related to movies at all and it's some freak circumstance, you *know* your first film is going to have huge flaws. Your first anything is. If it doesn't, it's dangerous to you in some ways. But I really honestly felt that I had done a good job on the film. Almost all the way through . . .'

★ ★ ★

Nicholson had to edit *Drive, He Said* at weekends, because during the week he was back in his actor's garb, making *Carnal Knowledge* with director Mike Nichols. This film, though immeasurably more successful on a commercial level, was decidedly inferior by any other standards.

The idea of following two young men's adventures in sex from college to middle age, and of using their parallel odysseys to explore the 'American relationship', was quite promising, but it needed people of real talent to bring it off. Nichols, whose credits included *Who's Afraid of Virginia Woolf?*, *The Graduate* and *Catch-22*, was considered 'highly talented' by Nicholson, but neither *Carnal Knowledge* nor their later co-effort *The Fortune* was to offer any confirmation of this assessment. Jules Fieffer, who wrote the screenplay, was considered a very talented cartoonist by many, despite the fact that his thousands of cartoons seemed to revolve around two or three ideas. His characters, Charlie Browns and Peppermint Patties grown up and traumatized by sexual inadequacy, are all bitterly aware of being bitterly aware of being bitterly aware. They are not carnally knowledgeable, merely carnally obsessed. And so is the film.

Jonathan (Nicholson) and Sandy (Art Garfunkel) are two college room-mates in the late forties, and in between talking and dreaming sex, actually come across a real live female, Susan (Candice Bergen). Sandy becomes her friend and longs for her body,

87

Jonathan gets the body but yearns to be her friend as well. So sex and love are neatly separated, and this first section creates the basis for what could have been a thoughtful film. But, alas, love has been separated only to be cast aside as ideologically irrelevant, and the next time we meet our two heroes they each have a perfectly honed sex-object in tow. Sandy has the buxom sweetie (beautifully played by Ann-Margret), Jonathan the all-American 'ball-buster' (Cynthia O'Neal). This isn't a satisfactory arrangement so they swap, although by this time it's quite obvious that Sandy does need a buxom sweetie and Jonathan's balls are ripe for busting. The sweetie then attempts suicide because Jonathan won't marry her, so he does. Another ten years pass and they're now long divorced; Sandy, meanwhile, has acquired an apparently mute hippie-girl. Jonathan shows them a slide-show of his conquests which nobody seems to enjoy very much. The movie's last scene has him paying $100 for an erection skilfully engineered by a prostitute (Rita Moreno). So much for the American male, and, for that matter, the American female.

Since *Carnal Knowledge* was supposedly a 'movie for the times', a probing look at the problems it gleefully wallows in, it must be asked whether the characters portrayed are typical of the society and times they are being used to condemn. The answer is no. Doubtless there are a few Jonathans and a few more Sandys out there pursuing lives of Sisyphean sexuality, but to imply, as this movie does, that American males never stumble upon a satisfying carnal experience – if you do, then you're kidding yourself – is simply ludicrous.

In *Carnal Knowledge* all the characters are pathetic, in the worst sense of the word, and this loading of the deck seems to say more about the film's makers than it does about the world they are making films for. To make a film about people's problems, their illusions and anxieties and inadequacies, you need more than a slick way with a camera and a nose for the quick, vicious laugh. You need a bit of compassion. Otherwise, as Paulene Kael wisely commented, you end up with 'a neon sign spelling out the soullessness of neon'. What you don't end up with is a furthering of carnal wisdom.

★　　★　　★

Nicholson's next project, *A Safe Place*, had only one thing in common with *Carnal Knowledge* – a lack of quality. Henry Jaglom, who wrote and directed it, was one of the BBS crowd; he had acted in *Psych-Out*, *Drive, He Said* and *The Last Movie*, edited half of *Easy Rider*, and now it was his turn to direct something. In his own words, 'I came to New York, where I'm from, went to the Central Park of my mind, found Orson Welles, seats, Jack Nicholson, squirrels, Tuesday Weld, chessplayers, Phillip Procter, crackerjack, Gwen Welles, rowboats, Dov Lawrence, merry-go-rounds . . . Friends. Myths. Images . . . I put them all together, juxtaposed the realities, sank into the fantasies, tried to break through the myths, creating anti-myth, feelings, thoughts, vibrations. Painted my movie, changing colors and shapes as I went along, exploring childhood, loss, pain, loneliness, isolation.'

There was nothing slick and empty about *A Safe Place*. On the contrary, it wasn't slick enough and it was full of Henry Jaglom. Or, to be more precise, Henry Jaglom was full of it. As he put it himself, it was 'an internal movie instead of an external one'.

89

The story, such as it is, centres round young Susan (Tuesday Weld), who calls herself Noah – what else? – and, as my old mother used to say, thinks too much. Basically she doesn't like growing up, a feeling which the film finds not only understandable but also positively revolutionary in its implications. Every now and then Orson Welles appears as a jovial and rotund magician with a new cryptic truth to impart. 'Last night in my sleep I dreamed that I was sleeping, and dreaming in that sleep that I had awakened, I fell asleep,' he informs her with a perfectly straight face. She is *enthralled*.

Meanwhile, the world being the way it is, men come to trouble her, first the plodding, pragmatic Fred (Phillip Proctor), then the exciting, live-for-today Mitch (Nicholson). Neither has much to offer, especially in the way of cryptic stories. Nothing much happens in the usual sense, which is what the director had in mind, and nothing much happens in the emotional sense either, which is presumably not what he had in mind.

Some people liked it. The *Sight and Sound* reviewer thought the film 'delightfully, eccentrically funny. Most of the time, too, it is sad and yearning.' But most people were less impressed, and Gavin Millar summed up for the prosecution in *The Listener:* 'The self-congratulatory waywardness of the film is what is most offensive about it: that, while it is boring you to death, it thinks it is breaking new ground. Wind more like.'

★　　★　　★

The Hollywood 'New Wave' were not exactly setting the world on fire. Though several innovative and interesting films had been made – *Five Easy Pieces*, *Drive, He Said*, Coppola's *The Rain People*, Trumbull's *Silent Running*, to name but four – money-makers were definitely the exception. *The Last Picture Show*, directed by Bogdanovich, had been a commercial success, but despite earning some critical acclaim, was not much more than a soap opera shot in black and white. Dennis Hopper's *The Last Movie* had still not gained a commercial release, and *A Safe Place* might just as well have shared such a fate.

It was not simply that these movies were 'good-but-uncommercial'. They were full of good intentions, often possessed of a welcome and demanding complexity, but only *Five Easy Pieces* had come close to classic status. None of them would be carving niches in cinematic history, in the way that so many of the French 'New Wave' films had done.

The best, however, was still to come. *The King of Marvin Gardens*, according to director Rafelson, 'came about in much the same way as *Five Easy Pieces*. I do have a brother, and I felt that one of the relationships I was not able to explore at all in *Five Easy Pieces* was the one between the two brothers . . . I also had been a disc-jockey in Japan, and had been in the habit of doing long free-form stories on the air . . .'

Which is how the film begins, in a radio studio, with David Staebler (Nicholson) recounting the story of how he and his brother Jason had allowed their grandfather to choke to death on a fishbone. 'I think that at that moment my brother and I became accomplices for ever,' he says. The show over, he walks home through the dark Philadelphia streets, finds grandfather coughing with a virulent sarcasm, and ascends to his own room, there to weave further fantasies for his program, his life.

91

This bespectacled intellectual was an unusual role for Nicholson, and one that he reportedly needed persuading into. 'He wouldn't do the film unless I was in it,' Bruce Dern recalled with his usual lack of false modesty. 'Not because he wanted to give me a break but because he's not going to do another film for BBS and Rafelson unless he knows he's got an actor in there. In this kind of situation, if he's going to play a lame part he wants somebody in there, that he's going to do every scene with, who can make it look like it's really working.'

Dern, playing the up-vibe Jason Staebler, was more in character. It is he who summons David to Atlantic City, and opens the can of fraternal worms by embroiling him in his dream plans to buy up an Hawaiian island. The ties that bind the two brothers, and the differences of personality that forever hold them apart, form the core of the film. Each is in retreat from something: David seeks escape from the competitive world in his fantasy-life, Jason escapes from his inner self in frenetic, ever-optimistic wheeling and dealing. Neither of them is very successful; indeed, as someone wisely remarks towards the end of the film, they'd each be better advised to do what the other does.

Atlantic City is half illusion itself, its grandiose facade of palatial hotels sheltering the Mafia 'businessmen' who use it as a centre for their operations. Its streets, we are reminded, were used on the original American 'Monopoly' board, and the brothers' scheming, their lives, seem more and more like a game they can't stop playing. Only Jason's ageing prostitute-girlfriend Sally (Ellen Burstyn) manages to break through the circle of illusions. When it becomes clear that her young 'stepdaughter' has usurped her in Jason's affections she takes all her clothes and beauty aids down to the beach and burns them, crying 'no more competition'. This re-admittance of reality sets the scene for tragedy, and the film closes with David in the radio studio, for once telling a story that is true.

The King of Marvin Gardens has an interesting plot, but it is a film concerned with people, not events. The audience is given a few days in the lives of a few 'ordinary' Americans, an insight into their self-made dreams and self-made limitations. Nothing is spelt out but everything is there. It is not the sort of film that leaves you breathless, but it is the sort which returns in dreams. Superbly directed, written and acted, it is close to a masterpiece.

Those concerned knew how good a film they'd made. Bruce Dern thought it the best script he'd ever seen; 'It will be, without doubt,' he said, 'the best motion picture most people have ever seen.' Nicholson also predicted success. It was, after all, Rafelson's first film since *Five Easy Pieces*, Dern was 'a new and interesting actor', Ellen Burstyn had just been nominated for an Oscar, and he himself was 'as hot as I am, you know'.

But he'd also been in the business long enough to have his doubts. There were 'no heroics, an unromantic leading man'. The film was 'essentially reflective of a negative personal relationship': it could all add up to a 'completely non-commercial film'.

It did. Many people went to see it expecting another *Five Easy Pieces*, a movie full of vitality, humour and serious intent, and came away disappointed. There was nothing the film's makers could have done about that; the two films were bound to be connected in the public mind by the names of Rafelson and Nicholson, and they were bound to be profoundly different by the very nature of the subject matter. As Rafelson said, *Five Easy Pieces* was about the 'misdirection of energy', and therefore energetic, whereas *Marvin Gardens* was about the 'repression of energy', and therefore lacking in surface vitality. Those who went to see Bobby Dupea continue on his wayward way found no satisfaction in Nicholson's David Staebler, a man whose 'excitement' was all locked within. Some critics acclaimed the actor for not 'duplicating a previous portrayal', but such duplication was exactly what most of the public wanted. Nicholson, though fully cognisant of this, was nevertheless unrepentant: 'You can't expect an audience that is used to riding the back of a hero, or revelling in the audacity of the villain, to identify with these people in a conventional way. But at the same time, this doesn't mean that the film shouldn't be widely available to people who might want to see it. It's a process, really, of educating the audience as you go. On a panel I was part of recently we had a lot of questions about the actor's social responsibility. Now I think that the actor's social responsibility, more than supporting a candidate or something, is to support a film like *The King of Marvin Gardens*, which otherwise simply wouldn't get made. That is an *actor's* way of influencing the system; it is what we can do to help in educating people, which as we all know is finally the most important way of affecting society.'

He took the responsibility seriously, refusing to accept more than the minimum Actor's Guild rate for working on *The King of Marvin Gardens*, but few of his colleagues in the industry were aware that such a responsibility even existed. As far as the transnational accountants swarming through Hollywood were concerned, the 'New Wave' was no more than a box office failure; they were not in the business of subsidising art.

Certainly, the 'New Wave' writers and directors had over-estimated their audience, and Nicholson acknowledged as much. He agreed with Corman; 'the apparent advance of foreign movies in America' had come about 'quite simply because of their greater sexual explicitness.' It was a 'chilling point', but once American films had caught up in this one respect all 'the more sophisticated formal approaches to viewing narrative, to viewing character, to viewing observations about humanity' had evaporated.

It would be tempting to leave the demise of the 'New Wave' at that, were it not for the fact that a parallel re-separation of art and mass culture was simultaneously occurring in the field of rock music. Essentially, the sixties were finally over. There was no longer a massive market for explorers, lunar or loonie. There was no longer much of an audience for growth.

*   *   *

In some ways the ebbing of the 'New Wave' left Nicholson stranded on a familiar beach, a prey to the new transnational moguls and their 'ideas' of what a real movie should be. But in others his position was quite transformed; the relative unknown who had entered the 'New Wave's' brief light-between-tunnels in *Easy Rider* was now a bona fide star. Now they needed him as much, if not more, than he needed them, and the limits on his artistic freedom would be largely self-imposed. Largely but not

95

wholly, for the very fact of stardom would impose its own limitations.

What is a star? Someone whom the audience wants to see and whom the industry thus finds bankable? Partly. A star is someone whom the audience wishes to see doing and thinking certain things, someone who sums up, through a series of cumulative performances, an approach to contemporary reality which the audience can share. A star is a *social construction*, and as such a hostage to the society which has awarded the accolades. A star, according to Teresa Grimes, expresses 'social assumptions about sexuality, about masculinity and femininity, about codes of action, behavior and gesture. The expression of psychological, social and moral values are located within the figurehead of the star and symbolically worked out through generic patterns and the conventions of story, plot and character.'

For the actor or actress who still exists within the star the obvious and insistent danger lies in stereotyping. Stars have to be partially predictable; they can show off different facets of the persona they have come to represent, but they cannot easily abandon the persona altogether. Nicholson had come dangerously close to the latter with his portrayal of David Staebler, a character too far removed from the basic George Hanson-Bobby Dupea construction. He was aware of this, and would continue to worry about it, saying in 1976 that he was beginning to feel 'that if I don't play this kind of extremely vociferous, well-meaning lout the audience is not happy'. But he was damned if he was going to be trapped by it. Even though he knew that audiences didn't 'want to see me do *Marvin Gardens'*, he still wanted to 'try to do something different each time'.

David Thomson expressed the actor's problem succinctly: 'The appearance of Jack Nicholson will open us to all that is and has been Nicholson, like the unique combination releasing a lock. The cinema is about appearance, but stardom is a matter of consistent appearance – the same person and personality must turn up with Nicholson's face, whatever the inconvenience.'

There were two ways of loosening this straitjacket. One was to create a persona so rich and complex that a wide variety of roles could be accommodated within it. The other was to make movies that were equally complex, with directors' and writers who were as talented and distinctive in their own right as Nicholson was in his. A Charles Bronson-type star, who didn't much care if all his parts were cast in the same mold, could afford to dominate the making of his films. Nicholson, who did care, could not.

As regards his public image, Nicholson was kind enough in 1975 to attempt a definition. 'I think they believe that I'm fairly uncompromising, that I have a certain vitality about what I do, that I'm almost, at such an early age, iconolastic in my attachment for individuality . . . that I'm capable of making a horse's ass of myself because, for people who like me, I translate into a kind of honest vulnerability which comes from not attempting to solidify my position . . . I hope and believe that people sense that I'm honestly interested, though possibly more cynical than they'd like, about all of our lives.'

The most interesting thing about this self-image portrait is how much of both Bobby Dupea and David Staebler it manages to contain. It reflects a persona of great complexity, taking in both introversion and extroversion, idealism (or at least hope) and cynic-

97

ism, rigidity and flexibility, individualism and a social conscience. Teresa Grimes would reply that such a persona 'relates to contradictions in ideology', which it functions 'to hold in balance, disguising as it were the existence of such contradictions.' But if her analysis is correct, there seems no reason why the persona should not function in the opposite manner, as a continuing exposure of those contradictions. In Nicholson's case this seems to be exactly what has happened; he has used his multi-faceted image as a mirror to the multi-faceted realities of the society.

Of course, the media prefer simpler packages, and Nicholson has been labelled 'the new Bogart', 'the redneck hippie', and, most interestingly, the 'Mr Smith who has done drugs, the Mr Deeds who has learnt to accept corruption in high places.' Perhaps the best description, which emphasized both the continuity of, and the scope within, the Nicholson persona, came in a review of *The Missouri Breaks*. He brought to the role of Tom Logan, the reviewer thought, 'his own peculiarly compromised brand of Hollywood anarchism, seen at its most commercially strident in *One Flew Over The Cuckoo's Nest*, its most quizzically uncomprehending in *Chinatown*, its most institutionally frustrated in *The Last Detail*.'

Overall then, Nicholson seems to have escaped stereotyping of the worst kind. He has not become totally predictable. There are no 'Nicholson films' in the way that there are 'Eastwood films' and 'Bronson films'. No one, for instance, could accurately describe *Chinatown* as a 'Nicholson film'; it bears his mark as both an actor and an image, but it also bears the marks of Towne, Polanski, Faye Dunaway, Raymond Chandler, of the genre itself. Nicholson's persona is a part of the film, but it does not dominate it, does not define it.

Which brings us to the second straitjacket loosener, a choice of films and co-workers that would utilise rather than magnify the power of Nicholson's image. In this respect he has done all that he could and more. The list of directors with whom he was to work contains many of the world's finest and strongest – Antonioni, Polanski, Forman, Penn, Kazan and Kubrick. The list of co-stars would be no less glittering – Faye Dunaway, Maria Schneider, Warren Beatty, Louise Fletcher, Marlon Brando, Robert De Niro, Shelley Duvall, Diane Keaton and Warren Oates. All of these directors and many of the actors had their own 'auteurs' ticking over. They would bring out different facets of Nicholson's cinematic persona, just as he would help to enrich theirs.

7

DARKNESS
ON THE EDGE OF TOWNE

'Though I am a whore, I am a whore with principle.
Chinatown *is commercial but artistic . . .'*
Roman Polanski

NICHOLSON SPENT MOST of 1972 away from the
cameras, caught in a mesh of unwanted and/or abor-
tive projects. He had been wanting to work with
Michelangelo Antonioni for some years – the Italian
director had been the first person not directly
involved to see *Easy Rider* – and provisional agree-
ment on their collaboration in a project entitled 'Tech-
nically Sweet' had been reached in 1971. But Nicholson was not destined to play the crap-shooting cham-
pion who gets involved with a young girl; producer
Carlo Ponti was not satisfied with the projected

100

'Badass' Buddusky: *The Last Detail.* KOBAL COLLECTION

Looking for the new frontier with Dennis Hopper and Peter Fonda
in *Easy Rider.* KOBAL COLLECTION

The traffic jam as a personal insult. As Bobby Dupea in *Five Easy Pieces.*
KOBAL COLLECTION

Henry Moon and saviour. With Mary Steenburgen in *Goin' South*.
KOBAL COLLECTION

'Heeeeere's Johnny!' As Jack Torrance in *The Shining*. KOBAL COLLECTION

'People get hanged for that Cora.' With Jessica Lange in *The Postman Always Rings Twice*. KOBAL COLLECTION

'A quiet, deeply bitter man.' As Eugene O'Neill in *Reds*. KOBAL COLLECTION

budget, and the enterprise was abandoned. A similar fate befell *Une Larme, Un Sourire* which was to co-star Nicholson and Jeanne Moreau with Charles Eastman (Carol's brother) in the director's chair.

Over at Paramount, meanwhile, Bob Evans was attempting to cast *The Great Gatsby*. Nicholson had always expressed a yearning to play this part, and his reasons for turning it down remain obscure. It was variously reported that he didn't want to work with Ali McGraw, that he wanted too much money, that he had strong 'personal reasons' for refusing the role. The actor himself said that he 'wanted to play the part', but 'didn't want that film . . . I didn't like the way they were talking about it.'

He was approached to play one of the three leading roles in *The Sting*, but neither the script nor the part interested him enough. 'I knew I could do the part well, and I knew it might widen my appeal. But I don't know if I really want that at this stage. I'd still rather take different sorts of challenges than the one of becoming a bigger and bigger Jack Nicholson.'

At roughly the same time he was offered the leading young role in *The Godfather*, and one thing he really did want to do was make a film with Marlon Brando. But when it came to studying the script, Nicholson discovered that the two men would not be sharing a single scene together, and this decided him against. 'I thought, well, I'm liable only to get to work with Marlon once, and let's hope it might be something where we're really having to work together.'

More surprisingly, the actor reportedly flew to London with the intention of landing the lead role in Fred Zinneman's *The Day of the Jackal*. Perhaps Nicholson liked Frederick Forsyth's book, perhaps he admired and wanted to work with Zinneman, but the

101

tight-lipped Jackal would certainly have been a risky role for him to play. If audiences hadn't liked him as David Staebler, it seems unlikely that they'd have responded well to a clinical, psychopathic reprise of Staebler's introversion.

Disappointingly, he hadn't been overwhelmed with offers to direct, and had apparently lost the inclination to write. The only project he was personally pushing, and would continue to push through most of the decade, was a film version of Donald Barry's western novel *Moontrap*. It had, the actor thought, 'a good story, very strong human emotion and a hot edge of the tribal uncanny, which I think will make it unusual.' Too unusual perhaps. The money-men were uninterested.

★   ★   ★

Robert Towne has already been mentioned as Nicholson's old flatmate, a fellow member of Jeff Corey's acting class, and an actor in *Drive, He Said*. Like many of Corman's 'bright young men' he could turn his hand to most things cinematic, but his métier was screenwriting, and by 1972 he was well on the way to being established as one of Hollywood's most sought-after talents. His first credits had been for *The Tomb of Ligeia*, one of Corman 'Poeisms', and *Villa Rides*, a fairly awful western with, courtesy of Towne and co-writer Sam Peckinpah, a strangely literate script. Warren Beatty, Francis Coppola and Gerald Ayres had called him in to do partial rewrites on, respectively, *Bonnie and Clyde*, *The Godfather* and *Cisco Pike*. This was not a bad record by any standards, and it was soon to be greatly enhanced by his screenplays for Nicholson's next two movies, *The Last Detail* and *Chinatown*.

The former was based on Darryl Ponicsan's novel of

the same name, which came out to much critical acclaim in 1970. Gerald Ayres, an ex-bigwig at Columbia now producing independently, read the novel before it reached the printers and snapped up the rights. Looking for someone to share the screenwriting with, he fixed on Towne. Both men considered that the central character, Billy 'Badass' Buddusky, was ideal for Nicholson.

At least, this was the story the way Columbia told it. According to Nicholson he himself had seen the novel in proof form. 'It was when we were shooting *Five Easy Pieces*. I didn't have the money to buy it but the producer was a friend of mine. The director, Harold Ashby, was going to make another movie with me so we made this one instead.' Nicholson was particularly attracted by the idea of playing a 'professional person', something he hadn't done before. Ashby was presumably attracted by the fact that Nicholson's name would improve the film's chances of a large audience, something not shared by his first two movies *The Landlord* and *Harold and Maude*, both excellent flops in the fast-developing tradition of the Hollywood 'New Wave'.

The Last Detail follows the episodic journey of a convicted sailor and his two escorts from Norfolk, Virginia to the naval prison in Portsmouth, New Hampshire. The prisoner, a teenage recruit named Meadows (Randy Quaid), has been caught trying to steal forty dollars from a polio collection box – it happens to be the CO's wife's pet charity – and sentenced to eight years incarceration with a dishonorable discharge to follow. Buddusky (Nicholson) and Mulhall (Otis Young), the two life-service sailors detailed to escort him northwards, first resent the job and then come to see it as an excuse for a paid vacation. With seven days to deliver their package, they should manage to spend at least four in the big, bad cities of the eastern seaboard.

But the kid's plight and attitude gets to them. It's quite obvious that he's more of a kleptomaniac than a hardened criminal-in-embryo, and the severity of the sentence is equally clearly a gross miscarriage of Navy justice. The 'lifers' feel sorry for Meadows, feel outraged by both the injustice and the boy's lack of resentment of it. He isn't playing the game; he should, like them, be railing impotently against his fate. Still, he's just a kid, so perhaps it's not his fault. They decide to spend the week making a man of him, and in the process to leave him with some warming memories to carry through the years that lie ahead.

So the kid learns. How to answer back, how to semaphore, how to return his eggs when they're not just right, how to brawl, how to have 'fun', how to enter what Buddusky calls 'the wonderful world of pussy'. He learns so much that he tries to give his escorts the slip, thereby causing the enraged Buddusky to pistol-whip him. The movie ends with delivery done and the two lifers walking away down an empty street.

It's a film of episodes, many of them hilarious, and all spattered with the densest spray of foul language ever to hit the screen. But beneath the 'fun', the energy, the mood remains thoroughly bleak, and the sense of blasted lives extends far beyond the central fact of Meadows' victimization. The plot may place the kid's fate in the spotlight, but the film is ultimately more concerned with the situation of the two lifers. The kid's basically an innocent, a victim of the neglect apparent when the threesome visit his mother's bottle-strewn home. The lifers are the victims of the game they – and, by implication, most of us — play, the game that says you can bite the hand that feeds you so long as you don't draw blood. They know the sentence is absurdly unjust, but they're not about to jeopardize their own positions in a Navy they claim to despise by letting him escape.

For the black Mulhall this instinct for self-preservation makes sense; his choices have doubtless been circumscribed from birth. And, in any case, he seems more aware of the dilemma, telling Buddusky at one point that there is no middle ground; they have to either deliver or release Meadows, they can't have it both ways, salving their consciences by giving him a good time and then handing him over to the keepers of misery.

But Buddusky won't accept this, can't accept it, and his non-acceptance is the mark of the inner devastation which he represents and which lies at the heart of the film. Here we have an uneducated Bobby Dupea, but no less complex for the unorganised pattern of his self-beliefs. It is interesting to note that Towne actually re-wrote Ponicsan's Buddusky, moving him away from Dupea. In the book Buddusky is something of an intellectual, a secret Camus-reader with a beautiful wife in New York and a 'Whitmanesque appreciation of the sea'. Yet still the parallels remain. Towne's Buddusky, like Dupea, is a fountainhead of manic energy, doomed to misdirection by the lack of a commitment to anything save himself. Just as Dupea could neither stay with nor truly leave his family, was trapped within his alienation from it, so Buddusky can only come to terms with his own 'life sentence' in the Navy by leading a schizophrenic existence, on the one hand accepting the rules, on the other condemning those who do likewise and casting himself as the 'badass', the rebel. He's the man who shakes the bars of his cell in the belief that he's impressing the other prisoners.

He fits perfectly into, characterizes in the literal sense, the film's metaphorical picture of America, and Western society in general, as a giant institution dehumanising the humans it supposedly serves. No one wins in *The Last Detail*. Like so many of the movies being made in America during this period it epitomises the mixture of sadness and self-hatred which followed the souring of the sixties' dreams. As Towne put it: 'Without saying it, or trying to be pushy about it, I wanted to imply that we're all lifers in the Navy, and that we will go along and be helpful to someone if our kindness or our courtesy doesn't cost us too much and if it flatters our vanity. We'll get this kid laid, we'll buy him a few beers, we'll let him have a good time if that makes him think more of us, but we won't risk our neck. And all we'll do is feel a little guilty, and cover it up by saying "I hate this chicken-shit detail."'

Towne also added, interestingly in view of the problems to come on *Chinatown*, his views on the way the film ends. In the book Buddusky is killed, in the film his suffering is only psychological. 'I thought it would be dishonest to let the sailor off or to have the others feel so badly that they would go AWOL or get themselves killed. I also thought that this would let the audience off the hook. "Gee, we're not so bad. We let the guy go" . . . *The Last Detail* ends badly, but along the way there is a certain amount of warmth, friendship, good times, a concern for each other, people being decent. This serves to accentuate that in the end all those things go by the board: if there's going to be a tunnel at the end of the light, you want to have some light before you get there.' Ashby obviously agreed with him; Polanski would have other ideas.

The Last Detail has faults, many of them inevitable carry-overs from the novel. The story structure is contrived and feels it. You know there'll be the fight and the whorehouse scene and so on, with each piece guaranteed to elicit the appropriate emotional reaction. The musical score, for which Ponicsan could not be blamed, only emphasised this problem, pointing out the ironies of each situation with all the subtlety of a Michael Winner film. Most of this could perhaps be put down to Ashby's relative inexperience; certainly such weaknesses were not to be apparent in later films like *Being There*.

Nicholson's performance was showered with praise, and quite rightly so. Nevertheless one reviewer did offer an interesting, dissenting opinion. John Simon considered Buddusky just one more airing of the actor's 'customary turn, which consists of delaying the reaction time to most stimuli in order to accelerate it in one or two others, and letting the emotion either seep or hurtle to the surface towards a slightly exaggerated, distorted climax – sometimes even an overstated indifference. Most of this derives from Brando, and often misfires even for him. And one cannot get around the feeling that the basic pigment of all Nicholson performances is an impasto of smugness.'

Sticks and stones? Well, whether Nicholson took such reviews to heart or not, he could certainly afford to ignore them career-wise. He won every national acting prize on offer for Buddusky, with the single, glaring exception of an Academy Award. More important to him perhaps, he'd won the respect of the people he thought mattered when it came to judging a performance: 'Whenever this film has been shown, old Navy men have come up and said: "Yeah, that's how it was."'

★   ★   ★

Chinatown was Jack Nicholson's thirtieth movie. It was also, according to producer Bob Evans, the film that 'made Jack's career. It found him a character actor and made him a star.' And, last but not least, it was to prove a great movie by any standard, a tribute to the diverse talents which brought it into being.

The first of these, the instigator, was Robert Towne. He began developing the screenplay, at this stage no more than two characters in search of a plot, when Columbia postponed the filming of *The Last Detail* because of cold feet over the language and explicit sex. Towne refused to soften the former, and Nicholson backed him up. 'Meanwhile, I conceived a detective film because I wanted to direct. I thought that no matter how bad a director I was, at least if I could tell a detective story I could keep people interested.'

The story came together slowly, woven from a number of disparate threads. Towne wanted the action to take place in Los Angeles, having grown up in the city yet never written a screenplay set there. He remembered how certain areas had looked, and his memory was jogged by a photo-article in *West* magazine titled 'Chandler's LA' and featuring shots of 'then' and 'now'. He began reading about the city's history, particularly the fascinating story of the 1930s Owens Valley War between farmers and developers.

In a different corner of his cranium Towne was

108

evolving two characters, one of whom was to embody the enigma of the city's Chinatown district. A friend who'd once worked on the LA vice squad told him that that was the one area he'd not worked in – 'they really run their own culture'. Towne was not interested in the district, only in the state of mind, and he pictured a woman who would personalise it, who would be an insoluble mystery to the outsiders she inevitably came to fascinate.

Nicholson was also involved, more as an interested party than a co-worker, and Towne obligingly wrote in a role for him. Again it grew from a stray source, a newspaper article the screenwriter read about a divorce detective who inadvertently found himself embroiled in a farrago of political corruption. It was these two characters, and the title, which Towne explained over lunch one day to Bob Evans.

The producer, at this juncture, had other things on his mind. He was still up to his ears in the hassles surrounding *The Great Gatsby*, indeed, one of his reasons for lunching with Towne was to beg his help with the script. But, to his everlasting credit, Evans fell in love with the embryonic *Chinatown*. His then wife Ali McGraw seemed perfect for the female lead. He loved the title. And since Towne was 'busted at this time, really broke, I gave him some money to develop the story.'

While Towne was wading through Chandler, structuring his plot and writing dialogue, Evans signed a new deal with Paramount which allowed him to produce his own movies whilst remaining vice-president in charge of studio production. Unlike most of his contemporaries at this time he was a man prepared to take risks, as his backing for the notoriously unfilmable *Gatsby* showed. His choice of director for *Chinatown* was to be equally controversial. Roman Polanski's last two films, *Macbeth* and *What?*, had been anything but commercial successes, but Evans preferred to remember *Rosemary's Baby* and the Pole's long succession of critical triumphs in the sixties. *Chinatown* needed such talent.

Polanski loved the screenplay, but he also had reservations. The dialogue was fantastic, the visual interest insufficient. Towne disagreed, but to no avail. 'Look Bob, I'm taking over,' the director told him, and spent the next two months restructuring the scenario. The dialogue was left virtually untouched but the plot was greatly simplified, with characters being ditched right, left and center. Most importantly, Polanski changed the screenplay's angle of vision, putting it firmly in the Chandlerian mould; the audience would never know more than the detective knew. As for the end, he left that open. Inspiration would provide the answer when the time came.

By this time Ali McGraw had left Evans for *The Getaway* co-star Steve McQueen, and Faye Dunaway was offered the leading female role. Both she and Nicholson were to have more than their usual share of problems working with a director.

Polanski had a decidedly jaundiced view of Hollywood. The things he hated about the place can be readily inferred from the list of things he loved, 'this total improbability, this playing of endless children's games in an intellectual Sahara, a seductive place in which glorious child-toys called movies are made.' And he was somewhat paranoid. 'You are continually under attack,' he claimed, 'from your stars, crew and studio with its financial statements. I am publicly called by many of these a megolomaniac and they are absolutely right, you *must* be one to make a

110

good film! Because you *must* believe at all times that your decisions are utterly right – even when they're wrong.'

Such attitudes didn't make him easy to work with, and Nicholson was already laboring under the double burden of the film's first person perspective and his belief that the movie's success was crucial to his career. It was crucial to Polanski's too, and he insisted on giving Nicholson line-readings, a chore which didn't worry the actor until he found out that no one else was being asked to perform it. But there was no way he could get out of it. As he said, 'The bastard's my friend. What am I going to do? The little bastard's a genius.'

In her excellent *Polanski*, Barbara Leaming describes one particularly fraught episode: 'Nicholson grew edgy, worn down by the gruelling schedule and lack of response. Polanski exploded one afternoon at Nicholson's immersion in a basketball game on TV when he was supposed to be working. Polanski whacked the screen with a metal bar but it did not break. Turning red with anger, Nicholson tore off his clothes, right there on the set. Polanski's assistant tried to calm them down, but both men were too hysterical to go back to work. Instead Polanski had a drink and drove off in his car. Stopped for a red light, he saw Nicholson beside him, in his dilapidated Volkswagen. Nicholson grimaced, Polanski grimaced back, they slapped hands through the open windows, and drove off in different directions.'

Faye Dunaway had an equally difficult time. Mrs Mulwray was a hard enough part to play without Polanski making it harder. The director would explain nothing of how he saw the film or the character, and when Dunaway begged for some notion of her character's motivation Polanski simply screamed back that the money she was earning should be motivation enough. At one point in the filming he nonchalantly yanked a stray hair from the actress's head. She walked off and it took all Evans' tact to persuade her back.

*   *   *

Only the last scene of *Chinatown* takes place in Chinatown, but the physical and metaphysical tentacles of the place weave in and out of the story like an indefinable *Hound of the Baskervilles*. Chinese music tinkles away, Chinese servants scurry to and fro, Chinese prints and curtains adorn American walls and window-frames. All are material manifestations of what seems like a socio-psychic black hole, threatening, fathomless, yet with a power to attract which cannot be resisted. All roads lead to this Chinatown of the mind.

J J Gittes (Nicholson) used to work in the district when he was a cop, and the advice he was given, the advice engraved on his heart, was 'do as little as possible'. Now he's a small-time private investigator, far removed from such mysteries in his prosaic pursuit of compromising photographs for his cuckolded clients. He dresses with the required flash but he's no Sam Spade, merely, in Towne's description, 'persistent and insatiably curious . . . capable within certain limits'.

The film begins with the sound of vigorous love-making and photographs of the same. But, it swiftly transpires, the groans of ecstacy are groans of betrayal: another client has been successfully appraised of his wife's infidelity. Gittes sits there as the client rants, a finely judged mixture of professional sympathy and professional impatience. 'All right, Curly' he drawls, 'you can't eat the Venetian blinds. I just had 'em installed Wednesday.' The traditions of the genre are satisfactorily re-established.

Another client, who says her name is Mrs Mulwray, wants her husband's extra-matrimonial life looked into, and Gittes plunges headfirst into more than he usually bargains for. Though this Mrs Mulwray is not the real Mrs Mulwray (Faye Dunaway), the real Mrs Mulwray's husband does turn up dead. Attempting to discover why, Gittes has his nose split open by way of a friendly warning.

This, of course, doesn't deter him. A private eye's gotta do what a private eye's gotta do, and he's becoming more than interested in the mysterious Mrs Mulwray. Her dead husband was head of the city water authority, the city is suffering from a drought, and large quantities of water are apparently being diverted elsewhere. Behind all these shenanigans the figure of Noah Cross (John Huston), Mulwray's ex-partner and Mrs Mulwray's father, looms like a malevolent genie.

She's hiding something and Gittes is determined to discover what it is, convinced that her secret will explain the swindle which he knows is taking place. In fact the two have nothing to do with each other, except insofar as Noah Cross is the villain in both cases. Eventually he finds out that her closet-skeleton is the child she has had by her father, for whom the father is desperately searching. But, in the process of making this discovery he leads both Cross and the police to the child. He tries to help Mrs Mulwray arrange a getaway, but at their rendezvous point in Chinatown she is shot dead by the police. Cross has got away with the swindle, got away with killing Mr Mulwray, got back his incestuous daughter. Gittes, face to face with the dead Evelyn Mulwray, can only mutter 'as little as possible'. A friend leads him away, murmuring comfortingly, 'Forget it Jake, it's only Chinatown.' These final moments of *Chinatown* are bleak as bleak can be.

Twin themes run through the film, and these turn it into what both Polanski and Towne intended, an ideological updating of the *film noir*. One is the triumph of corruption, the other the inadequacy of the hero figure. There is no traditional denouement, no warming moment when the case is solved, the heroine saved, the villain brought to book. In *Chinatown* it is Gittes' solving of the case which ensures the triumph of villainy and the empty death of the heroine. As he says at one point to Evelyn, he once loved a woman and, in trying to help her, only made it certain that she would be hurt. In this and other respects *Chinatown* lays bare one of the major, painful findings of many in the sixties, that seeing through something doesn't necessarily change it.

Two particular scenes were the subject of bitter disagreement between Towne and Polanski. After Gittes and Evelyn have made love in the film she seems like a person temporarily reborn, and it's hard to escape the feeling that Polanski let his own attitudes towards women and sex interfere with his sense of character development. In Towne's version Evelyn had reacted quite differently; she was 'extremely upset and actually out of bed smoking. And Gittes was upset because he had just made love with her, and she was rejecting him. I think the original line was "Mrs Mulwray, I hope it was something I said". . .'

The other scene was the last. Towne again: 'Origin-

114

ally, I had Evelyn kill her father. Gittes tried to stop her but was too late. But he did succeed in getting her daughter out of the country. So the ending was bittersweet in that one person at least – the child – wasn't tainted. The one thing the woman had been trying to do – the purest motive in the whole film – was to protect her daughter. When she carried out this motive by killing her father, she was acting out of motherly love. You knew she was going to stand trial, that she wouldn't tell why she did it, and that she would be punished. But the larger crime – the crime against the whole community – would go unpunished. And in a sense that was the point. There are some crimes for which you get punished, and there are some crimes that our society isn't equipped to punish, and so we reward the criminals . . . there's really nothing to do but put their names on plaques and make them pillars of the community. It was this balance that I was looking for . . . my own feeling is if a scene is relentlessly bleak – as the revised end is – it isn't as powerful as it can be if there's a little light there to underscore the bleakness.'

Paulene Kael agreed with Towne that his was the logical ending, but Polanski, whom Kael dubbed a 'gothic-minded absurdist', did not, and there are strong arguments for his point of view. It is not Gittes' defeat, not even Evelyn's death, which sends a shiver down the spine at the film's end; it is the gargoyle grin of the triumphant Cross. To have killed him would have fatally weakened the impact. Polanski here was bringing together personal and social history with a rare sense of relevant vengeance; his wife Sharon Tate had been murdered in LA, a victim of the California dream run amok. And just as the Manson killings had capped the sixties, completing a circle and announcing the bankruptcy of 'doing your own thing in your own time', so *Chinatown* bid a far from fond farewell to LA as a city of angels. It was not simply, as Leaming says, that Polanski was 'perversely twisting' the detective genre; he was reflecting the perverse twist that had taken place in his own and American history.

Arguing over the plot apart, both director and writer had made splendid contributions in their own specialist fields. Towne's dialogue shines throughout, from the haunting last lines to the string of beautifully bad jokes. With the character of Gittes he had captured exactly the unheroic hero, the touchy, seedy detective who's 'sophisticated enough to be cynical about people' but who thinks there are 'limits as to how bad people could be'. Polanski, for his part, made the film a visual treat, resisting the temptation to move at a breakneck pace. His two favourite visual motifs – both of which can be traced all the way back to *Knife in the Water* – are skilfully sustained. Sex, which is about touching if its about anything, is always being watched or talked about. Water, the source of life and a means of death, flows through the film. The swindle is all about it, taps leak, radiators steam, two characters are drowned, one, apparently, in a puddle.

Nicholson too made a tremendous contribution. As an actor he greatly impressed 'the little bastard': 'You see how angry he gets in a scene? Unbelievably scary! He goes into a kind of fit, you don't know whether he is acting anymore! He is one distinct acting school, almost opposite to Stanislavsky. You build anger by getting it physically, pounding tables, people, it comes not mentally but by inducing it in your body,

116

with your body, take *that* you motherfucker . . . It can be very hard on you physically, it's hard on Jack, but what wonderful results.'

Polanski thought the best scene was the one in which Gittes lies down to go to sleep: 'Here is Nicholson's genius, here would be such a temptation to act for the camera which he never does, only for his internal self – anyway, he's in bed and finally we are going to get a breather, and the telephone starts, and keeps on and on. He doesn't touch it for minutes but you *know* he's going to have to . . .' The director also admired Nicholson's ability to think on his feet: 'We have a scene in which Jack attempts to light a cigarette and the lighter doesn't work. Good, he had the sense *not* to break the take, to just keep struggling with it, finally giving up, and what you've got there is something small, funny, wonderfully visual which you could never have planned.'

But it wasn't just acting skills which Nicholson brought to the part of J J Gittes. The detective is such a resonant character because he wears Nicholson's face. He's also Dupea and Hanson and Staebler and Buddusky, an amalgam of contemporary American archetypes. The film may be historically set in the thirties, but its psychologically set in the seventies, and it's no coincidence that in *The Last Detail* and *Chinatown* Nicholson plays characters with a great deal in common. Both Gittes and Buddusky sound more subversive than they are, deliver up innocents for punishment, end with a profound sense of failure. Gittes differs from Buddusky and other Nicholson characters only in terms of audience expectations. The private eye is supposed to be a hero, supposed to find justice where justice can be found. Gittes' failure in this respect is what makes him such a powerful figure of the times, and *Chinatown* such a resounding lament for worlds and heroes lost.

8

PROFESSION: STAR

*'A child of five would understand this. Send somebody to
fetch a child of five.'*
Groucho Marx in Duck Soup

A MAN, A westerner, in a jeep somewhere in an African desert. He's looking for a guerilla hideout, but no one is being too helpful. Villagers accept the filter-tipped cigarettes he flashes like alien ikons, but tell him nothing. A child guides him, nowhere. One of the guerillas, on a camel, clambers up a dune to show him something, sees a line of distant riders and promptly heads off for the desert equivalent of the tall timber. The man's landrover gets stuck in the sand. He hits it with a shovel, crying 'All right! I don't care!'

So begins Antonioni's *The Passenger* (*Professione: Reporter*), the film made by Nicholson in the gap between *The Last Detail* and *Chinatown*. He had long wanted to work with the Italian director, whom he considered 'the most influential film-maker of the last twenty-five years.' And he really had nothing to lose, for regardless of how successful or disastrous their collaboration turned out to be – opinions were to differ violently – it still offered the sort of experience he was never likely to get in America.

Returning to the film, the man, Locke (Nicholson) returns to his hotel. Wandering into the room next door he finds Robertson, a man whom he'd met and talked with the day before, dead on his bed. They look remarkably alike and, slowly, it occurs to Locke that he can switch identities with the dead man, can cut himself off from his own unsatisfying past and present, his wife, his adopted son, his job. He switches the photographs in their passports, moves the corpse into his own room, and sets off for Europe to keep the appointments listed in the dead man's diary. He's no longer stuck in the metaphorical sand.

He goes to London, then Munich, where he recovers some of Robertson's belongings from a locker: guns and a prospectus of arms diagrams. Soon after this he is approached by the head of the very guerillas he'd been trying to find as a journalist. Playing the situation by ear, he finds himself handsomely paid for Robertson's goods.

Meanwhile, his wife (Jenny Runacre) is becoming aware that something strange has occurred. She and one of Locke's colleagues (Ian Hendry) try to trace Robertson, assuming that he was the last person to see her husband alive, but slowly it becomes clear to them that, for some reason, Locke is masquerading as Robertson. Various remarks are dropped which illuminate Locke's alienation from both his family and his journalistic work.

In Barcelona, amidst the surreal splendor of the Gaudi-designed Hotel Mila, Locke finally meets the girl – 'The Girl' in the credits – he'd noticed in London's Bloomsbury Centre. She (Maria Schneider) helps him shake off the pursuit, now swollen by agents of the African government the guerillas are fighting. Heading south through Spain in a hired car they exchange cryptic comments about the meaning of reality and the reality of meaning and, needless to say, become lovers. She boosts his sagging sense of purpose and asks pertinent questions like, 'Doesn't it matter which side a gun-runner is on?'

Lying in bed in an Almeria hotel room he tells her the story of a blind man who recovered his sight, only to kill himself because the world was so impossibly ugly. Then he tells her to leave, and Antonioni's camera begins the seven-minute tracking shot for which the film is famous. Passing out through the barred window it encompasses the events taking place in the square beyond, the arrival of the government agents, the Girl walking, the arrival of Locke's wife, finally returning to the bed where Locke now lies dead. His wife, asked if she recognises the body, says 'I never knew him.' The Girl, asked the same question, simply says 'yes'. The camera follows a learner driver out of the square.

Because the alleged 'faults' of *The Passenger* are implicit in its alleged 'virtues', reaction to the film depends very much on which gains the upper hand in a viewer's mind. Anyone annoyed by the unreal ease with which Locke manages the identity-switch at the beginning was in for a rough ride, for at that sort of traditional, cause-and-effect, narrative level the film lacks any credibility. The coincidences multiply beyond rhyme or reason, making it quite apparent that the plot was simply being made up as a running afterthought, a sort of moving backcloth to what was *really* happening.

From this point of view the characterization looked thoroughly inadequate. All the major characters are tenuous to the point of symbolism, mere identities hung on the hooks of the odd stray sentence. Thus when Locke's wife says that he loved her, but that they weren't happy, we're supposed to create for ourselves the image of a relationship within which such a line makes sense. Alienation is assumed, not demonstrated or investigated.

The one thing that is made clear to the audience is the skill of the direction, and that, from the traditional point of view, is something which should not be apparent to the ordinary punter. Just as actors like Henry Fonda and Spencer Tracy were lauded for 'not letting the wheels show', so Hollywood directors are most praised when there's no apparent direction. Antonioni's seven minute shot in *The Passenger* runs directly counter to such traditions; it's so striking that it takes attention away from what is actually occurring within the frame, makes it obvious that we are watching a film, not life.

For Antonioni admirers, of course, all this is completely beside the point. A case could be made for building a sturdy narrative foundation before the taking of cinematic flight, but such matters are at best secondary. Locke is the key to *The Passenger,* and if he is recognizable, as a persona if not a person, then the film works at its own primary level. Everything else then falls into psychic place. The coincidences don't

121

matter because the plot doesn't matter; the film is about something else or, more precisely, a number of something elses.

It is about the hold of the past. Locke tries to escape his, but is killed by somebody else's. The Girl has no past, but she studies architecture, the freezer of history. His wife only comes to care for him when he becomes part of her past.

It is about distances, as all Antonioni's films are. The distance between the reporter and the reported, between the Third World and the developed world, between people and themselves, between people.

It is about the difference between reflection and action, about freedom and commitment. Its central figure is an actor acting.

It is about film, about the art of composition, the subversion of narrative structure, the ideology of the flashback. The seven minute shot is there because it's breathtaking, because it serves to unsuspend suspended disbelief, because it serves to tie all the threads of the plot together on a visual plane.

It is, in Antonioni's own words, about 'the myth of objectivity'.

It is, last and undoubtedly least, a 'thriller'.

Given all this, it doesn't matter a jot that The Girl carries only a handbag yet always has something different to wear. She's not a real person, she's a spirit, a reflection of all that Locke isn't. This film, to refer back to the Tanner quote used earlier, refuses to lead the audience, Hollywood-style, by the nose. It's there for the audience to wander through, picking up resonances here and there. It prompts questions which it refuses to answer.

Logically enough, Antonioni's refusal to feed his audience was reflected in his refusal to feed his actors. As Nicholson put it: 'He can't tell them because once he tells them, that's all he'll get. He'll get no input. His real function is to inspire input, and so fill up the outline of his images.'

Nicholson had never worked this way before and, according to the director, was initially 'rather lost. I use actors like elements of the image, which they are – sometimes the most important elements, but not always. They are used to having long talks with the director about everything, but I think it's not worthwhile to do this . . . I don't know if I succeeded, but I tried to bring Nicholson as close as possible to *my* character in the film, something quite different from anything he has done before.'

The actor went into more detail: 'Antonioni's basic approach to his actors is, "Don't act, just say the lines and make the movements." He doesn't make dramatic constructions, he makes configurations. And the simpler you can be, the clearer will be the configuration. If you mess the interior up, and so break up the interior part of your character, you will in fact be working at cross-purposes with him, because he is looking for clarity in that area . . . That was hard for me to learn, but I'm glad I did it.'

And did it well. Antonioni was full of praise for his American pupil. 'It wasn't easy for an actor like him, so professional, so conscious of the technique, the position of the camera. But he never makes a mistake, he makes any gesture seem natural.'

The critics thought so too. Derek Malcolm thought that 'no one could have held it together with a firmer focus'; Richard Roud that Nicholson struck 'just the necessary balance between reality and abstraction' that was needed to make 'the shadowy figure of Locke so effective.'

123

Nicholson had no reason to regret his trip to Europe. He'd been the person who got the project off the ground, using his star name to ensure its financial viability. He'd acted brilliantly in a manner to which he was not accustomed, worked with a director whose knowledge and skills he could hope to emulate in the future. As he said himself: 'Once you've been through a production with Michelangelo Antonioni, no one is ever going to throw you with strange moves, ever again.'

And, most surprising of all, he'd worked on a movie which not only stretched his talents, not only stretched the art of film, but also made money. This was the crowning glory. 'Let me tell you,' he triumphantly told Tag Gallagher in 1975, 'this film will make a small profit, and I'm fucking amazed about that, and I love the movie, the movie to me is fabulous. His [Antonioni's] success will make all those buildings on Fifth Avenue here where the big movie companies reside fall over with a total case of scleritis and ulcers.'

So there, Hollywood.

*   *   *

As the decade reached its mid-point, Nicholson's star was threatening to outshine all but the very brightest. His last four films had all been excellent and, with the exception of *The King of Marvin Gardens,* commercially successful. He shared the podium of superstardom with established crowd-pullers like Redford and Eastwood. His name meant money in a town where nothing much else counted.

His life had changed in more ways than one. He now had what Hollywood lawyers call a live-in companion situation, and ordinary mortals call a steady relationship, with director/actor John Huston's daughter Anjelica. They lived in Nicholson's house in the Hollywood hills, a secluded but relatively modest dwelling in a compound shared by actress friend Helen Kallianiotes and Marlon Brando.

Not that Nicholson spent much time lounging around the place. Though he kept telling interviewers that he wanted and needed a period of rest and reflection, 'time for the reservoir to fill up', his continuing impersonation of a workaholic was very convincing. Once a year he would fit in a visit to New York for a fortnight of hectic cultural refuelling; in a couple of days in the late winter of 1974 he and Anji managed to take in Joni Mitchell, the Ali-Frazier fight, an Art Deco show, a matinee of *Troilus and Cressida* and Bob Dylan.

There was no shortage of cash. Still, luxury might have him by the pocket but Nicholson was determined it would never get him by the throat. He remembered making $1,400 for the two westerns only too clearly; his current situation was all a little too incredible. 'I can't believe there are always chauffeured limousines waiting at my beck and call,' he would say in 1976, 'and that other people are always ready to pick up the check.' In the middle of an all-expenses visit to Tokyo, closeted with a Japanese masseuse who worked with her body rather than her hands, he thought to himself, 'Nicholson, this is all a dream. You're not a superstar . . . you're not being given the most exciting massage of your life by a woman all the men in Japan would commit hara-kiri for.'

But money had bought him his house in Aspen, Colorado, looking out over a vista of mountains and lakes. 'When I'm racing down one of those slopes,' he said, 'With the wind behind me and my body exploding with the speed of it all – I'll know I'm a human being again and not a superstar. That's reality, and it's also good for the sanity.' There were also less people ramming scripts into his face, less people on the look-out for spicy gossip for the Hollywood sour-grapevine. Locked away with Anji, and perhaps a few friends, riding the proverbial Rocky Mountain highs, he might also escape the shivers of insecurity that come with stardom. As he himself said: 'Once they want you, from that day you can be equally certain that at some time later they won't.'

★　　★　　★

A more paranoid man than Nicholson might have found plenty to concern him in the changes rocking the industry. He might be insulated from sudden destardom by the success of his recent films, but the Hollywood climate was definitely turning against those who wanted to make good, socially-conscious pictures. The 'New Wave' was fast becoming a matter for nostalgia, the corridors of cinematic powers were full of jostling young executives in designer jeans. Marijuana insights were out, cocaine thrills were in. The prophets hadn't been profitable enough.

While the 'New Wave' had been having fun on location, the money-men had been restructuring the industry, restoring its viability as an 'ongoing leisure retailing system'. They had been helped in this by the onset of the 'Great Recession' in 1973–4, which threw many of the smaller companies into the jaws of the majors, seven of whom – Paramount, MGM, Warners, Twentieth Century-Fox, Universal, Columbia

126

and the British EMI – now controlled most of the industry. These majors, like their counterparts in the oil industry, were diversifying as fast as they could. While Exxon bought up coalfields and researched solar energy, the film majors expanded their stake in television and other leisure enterprises. Movies were becoming a mere sub-division of companies they had once dominated, and like all the other sub-divisions their success was judged on the one and only criterion known to transnational corporations – profit. For them, as one wit put it, 'a notion supported by money is a concept, and a concept supported by money is an idea.' The definition of a good script was that Robert Redford liked it, because anything Robert Redford touched automatically turned into money.

There was no reuniting of the creative and business ends of the industry; the transnationals had not bought up the studios to make films, only to sell off the real estate and film libraries. The independents were still the film-makers, but their 'independence' amounted to no more than a free hand in making films the transnational philistines would agree to distribute. Films like *The King of Marvin Gardens*, unless they starred Redford *and* Streisand *and* Brando, were fast becoming virtually unmakeable. The audience was still mostly made up of the same age group, but the generation that fell into that group had changed, and doubtless some of its youngest members had been born at Woodstock. Already, as Neil Young wrote in one of his songs of this period, America was 'a million miles away from that helicopter day'.

The diversification programs also took their toll on the quality of the films being made. More and more the movies were seen as mere appetizers for ranges of tie-in products – clothes, toys, books, posters, records – and deep in the recesses of this brave new world it was hard to imagine tie-ins for a film like *Chinatown*, let alone for one like *The King of Marvin Gardens*. Sequels too were big business. They increased the turnover from the tie-in paraphernalia and, since the stars of such series were often contracted to make repeated appearances at pre-success prices, cheaper to make. As Nicholson's own star rose above Hollywood a very different creature was being born somewhere among the gadgets. The era of *Star Wars* was dawning. A new mass audience for spectacular crap was coming into being, attuned to a lush, technology-mad escapism. As the economies of the West (and, for that matter, the East) crumpled, there was always the hope that the Force was with you.

The respected French director Louis Malle summed up the situation as he saw it: 'What worries me is that the American film industry is totally mass-oriented . . . the trend now is to consider that if you don't have a blockbuster, you're nothing. In any industry, if your product brings in a twenty or thirty per cent profit, everybody is absolutely delighted. But in the movie industry if you don't bring in three hundred per cent you've done nothing . . . it looks like five pictures every year are going to hit the jackpot and the rest will be considered flops.'

The future was not all bleak, but it did seem as if a combination of luck, slick direction and an eye for the lowest common emotional denominator was attracting most of the money. Directors like Coppola, men and women with talent, a desire to make films about difficult subjects *and* a strong commercial sense, were fast becoming exceptions. This 'New Hollywood' belonged to film-makers like Steven Spielberg, Brian de Palma, George Lucas, Ridley Scott and John Carpenter, and their films, with a few exceptions, dealt in thrills rather than people. No matter how good such films as *Jaws* and *Alien* might be when judged on their own terms, the balance had been tipped too far in their favor. These films had a place, an important place, but they were beginning to dominate the industry, sucking up all its capital and demeaning much of its potential talent. It was no accident that only two of Nicholson's next ten movies would be directed by Americans from his peer group, and that one of these would be far and away the worst of the bunch.

*　　*　　*

His next screen appearance was in a movie which could have been dedicated to the new, corporate Hollywood. Based on a best-selling rock opera, directed by daring whizzadult Ken Russell, boasting enough big names to make the box-offices spin, *Tommy* had the lot. Well, almost. Admittedly it lacked depth, excitement, subtlety, characters or anything else that distinguished it from a glossy, two-hour commercial for the director and the music. You can't have everything.

Townshend's rock opera was always overrated in any case, partly because it exemplified rock's pretensions, partly because The Who, onstage, could make the slightest of material sound like driving magic. Turning it into a film only emphasized the emptiness of the 'philosophical' themes; rock is just another business, the film tells us, as if we hadn't noticed that records cost money. The sight of Russell himself, acting a cripple at Tommy's holiday camp in one of the later scenes, is a stern reminder that irony has its limits.

Nicholson's role in this extravaganza was mercifully small. He played a Harley Street specialist consulted by Tommy's anxious parents, and sings his contribution with all the panache that consigned his earlier efforts in *On A Clear Day* to the cutting-room floor. The actor thought he sang 'better than Oliver Reed', which was true enough but hardly grounds for satisfaction. He also added, thoroughly tongue-in-cheek, that he was available for touring, ruefully noting that 'all the American record companies are in the hands of friends of mine but not one of them has signed me up yet. I guess that's self-critical enough.'

*   *   *

It was a pity he didn't use the same faculties when it came to considering his next project. Stars have their weaknesses, and one of the most common among 'serious' movie-stars is a hankering to play the clown. It was Nicholson who brought the Carol Eastman script for *The Fortune* to director Mike Nichols, and presumably it was the two men who persuaded Warren Beatty, usually an excellent judge of projects, that he should take the other starring male role.

It's not really worth going into the plot in any detail. Suffice it to say that the film is set in the Depression years, that our two disreputable chums hit on the idea of securing the fortune of heiress Frederika Quintessa Bigard (Stockard Channing) by marriage and, when this fails, murder. The sets and locations were created to perfection; these and Nicholson's frizzy hair-do seem to have marked the extent of Nichols' ingenuity. Beatty and Nicholson, for all their individual talent, are not a convincing team, and the script, which even Newman and Red-

130

ford would have found hard work, proves the final killer. A few funny moments break the flat surface, but the overriding impression is of a Laurel and Hardy film minus Laurel and Hardy.

The Fortune also left rather a bad taste in the mouth. As the *Newsweek* reviewer commented: 'There is something hectic and ugly about watching a cad and a weasel trying to drown, however ineptly, an essentially defenceless innocent. *Fortune*'s balance is cock-eyed, and the romantic comedy genre itself, designed for lighthearted larking, is too thin to contain such an ultimately heartless vision of human relationships . . . a comic *Chinatown*, a moral wasteland of mean motives and faithless acts in which comedy cannot flourish.'

Why was it made at all? Quite simple, really. Because the stars wanted to make it, and that was the sort of motivation the corporations could understand. A film with Nicholson and Beatty couldn't flop that badly, no matter how awful it was. As the *New York Daily News* noted, the film was 'an expensive redundancy, a painful illustration of the limitations of the star system.'

Nicholson himself was disappointed rather than repentant. He thought that 'in all honesty the movie was lost in the editing, which is probably the most tragic place to lose it . . . I just think it's cut too short . . . It's cut like a movie that they're trying to get out in a hurry because they're not sure if they have enough story to carry it. That wasn't the case at all in my opinion.'

The actor has never been one to indulge in public criticism of his films, and this particular piece of self-justification should be taken with a grain or two of salt. *The Fortune* deserved to fail and did. Luckily for

131

Nicholson it would soon be forgotten, lost in the wake of his biggest success to date.

★   ★   ★

One Flew Over The Cuckoo's Nest was written, as a novel, by Ken Kesey in 1960–1 and published in 1962. Pre-Vietnam, pre-psychedelia, pre-Laing, it was a profoundly revolutionary book, one that influenced thousands of young Americans and helped to pave the way for the upsurge which followed later in the decade.

It was obviously ripe for dramatisation, and indeed, even before the galleys had dried, actor Kirk Douglas had purchased the stage and screen rights. He hired Dale Wasserman to adapt it for the stage and a six-month stint on Broadway followed in the latter part of 1963. But a film proved harder to produce, with one studio after another failing, for a variety of reasons, to get the cameras in motion. Wasserman sued Douglas over the screenplay rights, and though he eventually lost his case the whole project was stuck in legal limbo for several years. In the meantime Douglas sent a copy of the script to the Czech director Milos Forman, then still working in his own troubled country. It got lost in the Stalinist mail system.

By 1970 the discouraged Douglas was on the point of selling the screen rights when his son Michael offered to take them over, promising dad that he would at least get his original investment back. In the breaks afforded by his acting career – Michael Douglas is perhaps best known as 'buddy-boy' in *The Streets of San Francisco* TV series – he teamed up with Fantasy Records chief Sal Zaentz who, true to the

132

spirit of the times, was into product diversification. After watching a pre-release cut of *The Last Detail* they decided that Nicholson was perfect for the central part of McMurphy and, displaying a talent for picking talent which such temporary Hollywood cabals often lack, went back to Forman as their preferred director. According to Douglas they wanted the Czech because 'he is a realistic and a funny director. We knew we needed someone who could handle the comedy. He has a very delicate eye; a great ability to go from humor to pathos, sometimes in the same frame.'

It was an inspired choice, and the producers weren't through yet. They picked Louise Fletcher to play the appalling Nurse Ratched, and somehow stumbled on Will Sampson for the part of Chief Broom. Apparently the giant Indian was working in Mount Rainier National Park when a couple of men on horses appeared from nowhere and offered him a movie career. He wasn't to waste the opportunity, and before the decade was out he had gained the unique distinction of playing in both its best (*The Outlaw Josie Wales*) and worst (*The White Buffalo*) westerns.

The producers had less luck with their original choices of screenwriter and cinematographer. Kesey was all wrong for the former role; he was too close to the book and his insistence on retaining the novel's structure – with Chief Broom's first person narrative holding it all together – was deemed unacceptable. Lawrence Hauben and Bo Goldman were brought in to replace him. The eminent Haskell Wexler was chosen to hold the camera, but he and Forman could not agree on the desired approach. Wexler wanted to concentrate on framing and atmosphere, Forman was after a documentary-style realism, a more flexible approach. Wexler was amicably ousted in favor of Bill Butler.

Filming began in the autumn of 1974 at the Oregon State Hospital; the story begins with McMurphy's arrival at the institution. He's been serving time on a prison farm for assault and statutory rape, and the authorities half-suspect him of feigning madness to escape the onus of work. He quickly makes it plain that he intends to be a thoroughly unsettling influence on his fellow inmates.

This McMurphy is rather different to Kesey's. He's no 'spirit of macho' come to liberate his fellow-sufferers from the grip of the matriarchal 'Combine'. In some ways he seems like a Bobby Dupea who's been stopped from moving on, a Buddusky who's just heard that the kid hung himself in prison. But in both those characters there was more than a hint of self-culpability; McMurphy is a victim, pure and simple. He cannot hope to resolve his own problems while he remains in the power of the state. His anarchistic rebellion may be self-damaging but it cannot be self-defeating; it is, after all, the very condition of his survival as a human being.

The state is personified by Nurse Ratched. Kesey's amazonian matriarch has been transformed into 'organization woman', soft-spoken, prim, eternally self-righteous. She doesn't think she has a personal axe to grind; she's doing it all for your own good. Anyone who opposes her must, therefore, be doing her patients harm, and the word subservience doesn't seem to be in McMurphy's vocabulary. He introduces pornographic playing cards, argues over arrangements, questions everything. When the ward votes to watch a baseball game on TV and is over-ruled by Nurse Ratched, he sits in front of the blank screen, cheering the imaginary plays. And the others join in.

Next he hijacks the bus which is supposed to take them all bowling, turning the outing instead into an hilarious fishing expedition. When the authorities catch up with the boat several of the patients are proudly holding up their captive salmon. A sense of achievement, of self-realization, is bringing life to the patients and chaos to the ward. But Nurse Ratched remains confident that she can control the situation.

McMurphy then discovers that he, unlike most of his fellow-inmates, is committed until such time as the authorities choose to release him. He starts a brawl, and is sent for electro-shock treatment with the giant Indian, Chief Broom (Will Sampson), whom everyone assumes is deaf and dumb. He's not. Jerked out of his passive retreat by McMurphy's example, he agrees to join him in an escape attempt.

From this moment on the film's comedy slides further and further into tragedy. A farewell party for the escapees goes disastrously awry, with one of the patients committing suicide and McMurphy attempting to strangle the person he considers responsible – Nurse Ratched. He's taken away for more and harsher shocks, and reduced to a vegetable.

But it hasn't been for nothing. With his Christ-like sacrifice McMurphy has saved Chief Broom. The Indian smothers his wrecked friend with a pillow and flies the cuckoo's nest.

One Flew Over The Cuckoo's Nest is a film of two parts, both of them superbly controlled by Forman. The first half is funny without being played for laughs, the second cuts to the bone without sinking into pathos. No simple solutions are offered. We're never sure whether McMurphy is sane, but we are made increasingly aware that sanity is a rather elusive concept, too elusive for the state's peace of mind. The Nurse Ratcheds of this world like things clear-cut and shipshape, which makes them less attuned to reality than many of their patients.

Nicholson's performance received universal praise. Paulene Kael, after noting how easy it would have been for the actor to 'take over' the character, praised him for 'toning it down', offering the final accolade that 'you can forget it's Nicholson'. Derek Malcolm thought much the same: 'Though you can imagine a truer-looking paranoia, it is difficult to think of a performance that could be so riveting and yet so lacking in a star's insistence on blotting out opposition. Nicholson, unlike so many leading men, has an extraordinary capacity to fit himself round a part rather than wrap one conveniently around him.'

This was the key to Nicholson the star. If he'd just kept playing Bobby Dupea in different films there would have been no depth. And he knew it, so he didn't. Instead he played a succession of different characters, was a good enough actor to make them different even while his persona worked to connect them, to build them into a cumulative figure. He had the talent to have it both ways, actor and star.

One person with first-hand experience of working with him was, of course, Forman, and in 1976 he gave a remarkable tribute to Nicholson which deserves to be quoted at length. Nicholson had become a star, the director thought, 'probably despite everything and everyone. The moment he begins to work he becomes a servant; he knows the story, he knows the film, he arrives each day prepared to perfection, he is interested in an excellent ambience and he helps to create it. In a totally natural way he assumes the same discipline as any other actor. And he even has a tendency to assume more for he knows that it will make him still better. He is perhaps the only one of the great stars of today – with the probable exception of Marlon Brando – who isn't afraid to take risks. Whoever becomes a star begins immediately to repeat well-tested "sure things". He takes on every strained trick, he runs back to the sure ways which have won him his star status. With Jack it is the opposite. He gives you back the possibility of making a film and not photographing a star. He doesn't demand any privileges; he doesn't tell anyone how to photograph him, what angle to take etc. He literally has a horror of selling guaranteed qualities. To get him to show his smile, that's a real struggle. The fact that he took such a long time becoming a star has contributed to the fact that today he is a professional almost beyond human possibilities. One can shoot the same scene with him when he first recites a written text, then improves on it, and then attempt to fix the improvization. It is all equally true and spontaneous.'

Forman was not the only one impressed. At last, in 1976, Nicholson received Hollywood's highest honour, an Academy Award for Best Actor. How much it meant to him only he could know, and judging from the contradictory remarks he had made over the last few years perhaps even he wasn't sure. One thing was certain though – no actor had ever deserved it more.

9

ORDINARY OUTLAWS

'People also rob banks for money'
John Huston

The Missouri Breaks begins with the public lynching of a rustler, conducted as an exercise in deterrence by local pillar-of-the-ranching-community David Braxton (John McLiam). Unfortunately for him, the dead man's colleagues are not deterred, simply spurred to improve their mode of operation. A ranch of their own, they decide, will make it easier to relay their ill-gotten gains, and to pay for it they rob a train.

One of their number, Logan (Nicholson), stays to look after their new holding while the others head north across the border to steal horses from the Cana-

dian Mounties. Braxton meanwhile has hired a 'reg-
ulator', Lee Clayton (Brando), in an attempt to solve
the rustling problem once and for all. While Clayton
watches the world, and particularly the suspicious
Logan, through his high-powered binoculars, the latter is becoming romantically involved with Braxton's
daughter Jane (Kathleen Lloyd) and his comrades are
successfully carrying off their rustle.

Or so it seems. Clayton intercepts one of them,
kills him, and leaves his signature – a Sharps car-
tridge – in the headstall of the dead man's horse.
When Logan hears the news he goes after Clayton,
finds him defenceless in the bath, but cannot shoot
him in cold blood. He decides the gang will take
revenge on Braxton by stealing all his horses.

They manage this, but after splitting up for the
purpose of selling the mounts, are picked off one by
one by the seemingly ubiquitous Clayton. All, that is,
except for Logan, whom Clayton is deceived into
thinking has perished in a fire. He realizes his mistake rather abruptly, waking suddenly to hear Logan
say, 'Do you want to know what woke you? Lee,
you've just had your throat cut.'

An ordinary enough plot, perhaps. But there's certainly more going on here than meets the plotter's
eye, as a closer investigation of the opening scenes
makes evident. The rustler who is about to die
exchanges words with Braxton as they ride up the hill
to the hanging-tree. 'It's a beautiful country,' Braxton
says. 'Yes it is,' the rustler replies. Once the noose is
in place, the rancher courteously asks the condem-
ned man whether he would like to start the horse
himself. 'I will, sir,' he says, and does. It is as if the
whole plot of *Easy Rider* had been run through in a
couple of minutes.

Back at their ranch, Braxton and his daughter argue with each other. He doesn't fulminate against rustling in moral terms, he simply counts its commercial cost, seven per cent to be precise. He's not an evil man per se, just a businessman. Jane, though, refuses to see things in such terms, and it is through her eyes that the corruption implicit in them is made tangible. All that remains is to tie together corruption and culture: Braxton first asks his daughter to forget about the lynching, then asks her to hand him down his copy of *Tristram Shandy*.

It is a literate film, a film full of literate characters. Or perhaps intimations of literate characters. Clayton is the most outlandish, a burly, perfumed fop who kills people at half-mile range with his Creedmore rifle, an urbane sadist who likes stopping to admire sunsets. He thrives on his own eccentricities, talks a calculated mixture of whimsy and threat. He is, in director Arthur Penn's estimation, one of the 'crazy ones' called forth by a degenerate political system in its hour of decay.

Logan is a more rounded figure, one who develops as the film goes on. Jane brings out, and begins to ameliorate, his distrust of women he hasn't paid for. Looking after the ranch while the others are away brings out his long-suppressed urge for a place of his own. 'My people always wanted a place,' he tells his friend Cal, 'and since they were good people I always saw it with their eyes, you know.'

Jane Braxton is not the normal 'romantic interest', stuck in the middle of a western to look good and give the hero something to use and/or win over. In fact she seems the most intelligent and most perceptive of the leading characters, a point not missed by Betsy Erkkila, who wrote in *Cineaste* magazine that her part constituted 'a major breakthrough in women's roles in the American cinema'.

And yet, there is something fundamentally flawed in *The Missouri Breaks*, something that it is hard to put one's finger on. It is an interesting film to film buffs; it couldn't help but be with two of Hollywood's most fascinating actor-stars, one of Hollywood's most interesting directors, and a good script. If it wasn't a success, it would at least be an intriguing failure.

But which? Brando's performance was described as 'self-indulgent', 'incongruous' and 'breathtaking' by different reviewers. One, Richard Schickel, tried to have it both ways: Brando stole the film, but only because he was 'the only one connected with it to see that it was a load of nonsense and that the only honorable course was to send it up.' Nicholson was described variously as 'miscast', 'unfairly overshadowed', and 'marvellously subdued, burrowing from within to create a real, vibrant character which almost totally eliminates the star presence of his recent, flashier roles.'

And the critics were not the only ones trying to have their film and eat it. Penn, asked why he made *The Missouri Breaks*, said: 'It was Nicholson and Brando. I just couldn't pass up a chance like that. You know, you make so few movies in the course of your life, and so many of them have to do with nursing actors through them, that when you get a chance like this to go with two really superb heavyweights, why not go for them, if for nothing else than to be present and participating in it. That's why, in a sense, there is no thesis in this film. It was much more an event. And it certainly shows, I think.' The director told one interviewer that he was 'stunned by the seriousness with which it is being greeted.'

Still, that didn't stop him trying to explain the non-existent thesis. *The Missouri Breaks* was about 'a phase of colonialism . . . the colonialists, in the form of Braxton, have been overthrown, leaving behind no real community, no real political purpose.' It was, he told another interviewer, a 'metaphor for the modern world'. And there was no shortage of erudite analyses from the director's many admirers and interpreters. The western represented an attempted 'autodestruction of generic codes'; like Penn's recent *Night Moves* it reflected the American inability to form a counter-society. According to Penn's filmographer Robin Wood, it was simply one more in a line of films dedicated to the undermining of Hollywood myths. *Little Big Man* had debunked the US cavalry, *Night Moves* the private eye, now *The Missouri Breaks* was demythologizing the gunfighter as an heroic defender of frontier civilization.

And it is true, all these things *can* be justifiably read into the film. It is, at one level, a serious look at something. It doesn't rely only on the resonance of past performances by stars and director. But, and this is probably the most interesting thing about *The Missouri Breaks*, it is still not a good movie, and for reasons that were to a large extent outside the control of those who made it. First and foremost, audiences went to see it expecting too much. The reputations of Penn, Brando and Nicholson led people to believe the blurb; this *would* be one of the greatest westerns ever. This would be *On The Waterfront, Bonnie and Clyde* and *One Flew Over The Cuckoo's Nest* all rolled into one, a surfeit of riches, a synthesis of all that was best in the Hollywood cinema of the last quarter century.

And what did they see? Brando playing an extravagant loony, Nicholson playing someone restrained. The two great keepers of the Hollywood cinematic conscience trading jibes about rustling. There was no tension in the film, and Brando and Nicholson were normally actors who quickened the pulse, set the nerves on edge.

Many blamed Penn for this lack of intensity. If he'd decided to make a film which was 'intensive' rather than 'extensive', they argued, then it had to be tightly structured. As it was the film rambled, from the outlaws to Logan and Jane to Braxton and Clayton and so on. Nicholson, in retrospect, agreed: The film wasn't 'tied together enough . . . inside the episodes you lose the progression because the episodes are too protracted.' And one major reason for this was the lack of a finalized shooting script.

Which brings us back to square one, the movie's initial conception. Brando wanted to make the film because he was 'broke', and he needed money for the environmental experiments he was setting up in Tahiti. Nicholson wanted to make it because he wanted to work with Brando, Penn because he wanted to work with the two of them. And, like a brief break in the clouds, a period of time appeared in which all three were free of other commitments. The problem was that the period in question was only a few weeks hence. As a result everything had to be done in a rush, the locations scouted from the air, the costumes designed and made at breakneck pace. There was no time for any in-depth discussion of the script. There was none of the exhaustive preparation for which Penn's projects were noted.

At the time, this doesn't seem to have over-concerned the director or his stars – they were too involved in the mechanics of the thing – and it certainly didn't give the producers any sleepless nights. They'd paid $1¼ million for Brando and $1 million for Nicholson because they knew that those two names would guarantee the recouping of their investment. The quality of the film, within certain limits, was neither here nor there. If it had to be made in a rush, then it had to be made in a rush.

So *The Missouri Breaks* ended up a film made by brilliant people off the top of their heads. It couldn't help but be interesting, couldn't help but be half-good. And it couldn't help but leave the impression that it should have been so much better considering the talent involved.

Interestingly, while Brando, Nicholson and Penn were making a superior sow's ear out of a potential silk purse in Montana, Clint Eastwood, a lesser actor and director, was taking the time to turn a book he loved into the western film of the decade. *The Outlaw Josey Wales* was not only more exciting than *The Missouri Breaks* in the traditional sense, it was also funnier, more thoughtful in terms of contemporary American relevance and more innovative in its resolution of the western hero's traditional dilemmas. It was the heavyweight movie that the heavyweights had failed to deliver.

★　　★　　★

Nicholson must have been disappointed in the film, especially since he had thought in mid-film that 'a major classic' was in the making, but it had been important for him to play a role which bore little resemblance to the string of extrovert louts he was famous for. His Tom Logan possessed an inner strength wholly untypical of the Dupea/McMurphys

144

of this world, and added another notch to his already high reputation as an actor.

He had worked tremendously hard for that reputation, bringing to each of his roles a thoroughly professional commitment. He might appear spontaneous and easy-going on the screen, but that spontaneity was the result of considerable thought, technique and emotional effort. None of the directors he had worked for had had reason to complain about Nicholson's willingness to give himself to a role.

Polanski thought that Nicholson's approach was the opposite of the 'Method' approach, and Penn enlarged on this, contrasting him with Brando. The latter, Penn thought, 'feels out the drift of a scene and more or less *goes* with it. Nicholson is more organized. He knows where he wants a scene to go, while Brando doesn't *want* to know where it's going.'

Nicholson partially confirmed and partially denied this assessment in an interview given in 1975. He didn't go into a scene 'thinking "this character should be sad". I go in knowing he wants this, and the environment is that, and this is how he's going to approach his problem, and I try to make it even more important than it would be to the character, and that creates feeling. Whatever feeling trying to achieve those ends creates, that's the emotion. In acting, it's best when you don't really know. Unpredictability is the most arresting quality that an actor can have. It's as important to an actor as colour sense and line are to a painter.'

So rather than dig himself into a character, Nicholson digs an idea of his character into situations, and this 'halfway Method' approach perhaps helps to explain his success. By refusing to be swallowed up, as Method dictates, by a psychological reality, he is

145

allowed to remain, at least partly, 'Nicholson'. But by allowing the non-'Nicholson' part of the character and the situation to push him forward he creates his own unpredictability, and a total character who is both distinctive and familiar. He is never 'Nicholson' in the sense that Eastwood is always 'Eastwood', but neither is he ever subsumed by characters in the way that such fine actors as Bruce Dern and Robert Duvall are. His, in a way, is the classic Hollywood style realized by actors like Spencer Tracy and Henry Fonda. Both these stars were to some extent trapped within their screen identities, but in both cases that identity was elastic enough to contain a wide range of parts. Nicholson's range is perhaps not quite so wide, but there seems no reason why it should not become so. His performances in *The King of Marvin Gardens* and *The Missouri Breaks* proved he had the range as an actor, if not yet the range as a star.

He'll get there though. The one facet of Nicholson's personality which shows no sign of being affected by success is his intense curiosity, his unquenchable desire to learn. Which other stars of recent times have switched from good director to good director with such facility, and with such obvious forethought? He wanted to work with the best, with Antonioni and Brando and Kubrick. And he wanted to work even with those of whom he wasn't sure, like Russell, because there might be something there to learn. There has been something essentially calculated about the way he has 'planned his career', a feeling that he has always known where he wanted to go, and that Hollywood or no Hollywood he was going to get there.

Hollywood stardom might be a blank check, but Nicholson was still not making purchases he didn't need. He could have done a 'Bronson', made four films a year at $1 million a throw, milking his image into the ground. But he wanted to make 'serious movies', movies which by any broad definition could be termed political, movies which dealt with 'real human problems'. He wanted to give his audience 'fun and boils', films which entertained while they asked questions. He wanted to teach, and like any good teacher he knew that his first duty was to learn.

*　　*　　*

Elia Kazan was one of the better directors with whom he'd not yet worked, and missing *The Great Gatsby* was still one of his great regrets, so it came as no surprise when Nicholson agreed to take a cameo role in Kazan's film adaptation of Fitzgerald's *The Last Tycoon*.

The novel was unfinished, but unfortunately the film wasn't, surviving to offer further proof that Fitzgerald's genius with words was not easily transferred to celluloid. The book is about two separate things, connected in the author's head and the life of his central character: the way the Studio System spins its dreams and the way grown men reach for the unreachable woman. Kazan and screenwriter Harold Pinter faithfully followed Fitzgerald in giving pride of place to the second, mistakenly assuming that the author's haunting prose, which alone gives any substance to his adolescent obsessions, would survive the journey. Unfortunately a beautiful actress walking barefoot in wet grass sounds more haunting than it looks, and much of the movie ended up resembling one of those misty hairspray commercials.

The machinations of the studio executives are

147

rather better observed, with Robert De Niro giving his usual excellent performance as the obsessed Monroe Stahr. Nicholson's main scene, an argument-cum-brawl between his communist union leader and Stahr, is one of the best in the movie, and the actor was pleased to have played 'the first sympathetic communist in the history of American movies'. Anjelica also had a small part. But all in all *The Last Tycoon* was a star-studded failure.

★   ★   ★

It was now six years since Nicholson's first, and so far only, stab at direction. For several of them he had been working on the cinematization of *Moontrap,* and one company had now reportedly put up the necessary cash for the film to be made. But, according to Nicholson, 'some of the people behind it just weren't straight with me. I felt a little betrayed actually, because originally I was told I could direct it, but ultimately what it came down to was that if I would be in the film I could direct it and if I wouldn't then I couldn't. So with *The Shining* coming up, the only way I could get to direct something quickly was to star in it myself. I thought it was time for me to get away from big bombastic things, and I thought it would be a big challenge for me to make a romantic western comedy. Something that wasn't aimed right down the breadbasket.'

Goin' South was another property he had owned for several years, and one moreover which contained a part he wanted to play, the vulgarian no-hoper Henry Moon. Since the storyline centers around the relationship between him and the woman who saves him from the gallows – it's a kind of *African Queen* set

148

out West – the casting of his female co-star was of
crucial importance. Jane Fonda was the actress
Nicholson wanted, and it's easy to see why, but for
some reason the deal fell through. Fortune smiled on
the director nevertheless; walking into Paramount's
New York office he found one Mary Steenburgen, a
young actress who'd not yet earned a penny from her
chosen career, but who rapidly convinced Nicholson
that she was ideal for the part. The studio didn't like
it – 'why can't this man do anything regular?' the
executives whined – but Nicholson was adamant.
'What is stardom for if you don't take chances?' he
said. Steenburgen was both a challenge and an
opportunity. Everyone likes to be a starmaker, and
besides 'in a way I wanted someone who could teach
me something about the job.'

Another newcomer to the big screen was John
Belushi, whose brief career as Hollywood's favorite
low-life jester began on the Durango set. For the rest
of the cast and crew Nicholson relied on tried and
trusted talent. Christopher Lloyd and Danny de Vito,
who'd played minor roles in *Cuckoo's Nest*, and who
were both to find national fame with the TV series
Taxi, were added to the film's gallery of grotesques.
Nestor Almendros, who'd recently won plaudits for
his work on *Days of Heaven*, was chosen as cinematographer; Harold Schneider and Harold Gittes, two of
the old BBS crowd, co-produced. It was, in the jargon
of football managers the world over, 'a nice blend of
youth and experience (Brian).'

From the very first scene of *Goin' South* it was
obvious that Nicholson had learnt a lot about
direction since his last stint behind the cameras.
Henry Moon is trying to get his horse moving, does
so, and then rides away from the camera into the dis-

tance. Just as he disappears from view a posse goes galloping past the camera in pursuit, smothering the screen with dust. It's a neat inversion of the traditional opening – the hero usually rides *towards* the camera, looming into focus – and it's shot Antonioni-style, in one long take.

Henry Moon is caught of course – he's the sort that always is – and taken back for a communal hanging in the friendly town of Longhorn. There his catalogue of woes continues to unfold. His gang won't try and rescue him because it's too risky, and we find that this is not the first time that people have doubted his indispensability. His curriculum vitae is hardly impressive: a cook for Quantrill's raiders, a failed applicant for the Younger Gang. Nobody loves him but his girlfriend Hermine, who tearfully tells him that he was 'the best I ever had . . . 'cept maybe that circus fella'. Moon reciprocates the feeling in his own, inimitably romantic way later in the film: 'I'll never forget you Hermine. You was the first woman I never paid for.'

Fortunately for our hero the area has been shorn of marriageable men by the Civil War, and any man can be saved from hanging by a proposal of marriage. One old woman is desperate enough, and the exultant Moon whirls her round in the air. She drops dead. 'This just ain't your day Moon,' sneers one of the grotesques.

But it is. Young, attractive Julia Tate (Steenburgen) needs a man to work her secret goldmine and Moon is all that's available. They're married on the spot and she drives him off, rather like a relieved serf, to her place in the mountains. The camera pulls back to reveal a strikingly beautiful panorama of hills and sky. 'Well Julia,' says the ever-sensitive Moon, 'it ain't much but it's a start.'

This was Nicholson's favorite joke in the film, but there are many others, in many different comic modes, which are just as good. As Moon and his bride try to cope with marriage, sex, Moon's gang and the wicked railroad bosses, an anarchic comedy of rare vintage unfolds. Certain scenes, like the bloodless shoot-out between rival gangs in one room, are pure slapstick, and would not have seemed out of place in *Blazing Saddles*. Others come close to silent comedy, others again fuse a sense of social history with thoroughly modern satire.

But, and this is what makes *Goin' South* such an excellent film, the comedy is not allowed to take over completely. It may be a farcical *African Queen*, but it remains an *African Queen* nevertheless, touching as well as outlandish. There is nothing heartless or nihilistic about *Goin' South*; it has an underlying warmth reminiscent of the older Hollywood days, and none of the cruelty found in much of today's 'game for a laugh' style humor.

The film can also be seen as an extension of the 'relationship part' of *The Missouri Breaks*, with Julia Tate as a more developed version of Jane Braxton. This time round it is the relationship which forms the film's primary level, the corrupting influence of business the secondary level. Neither is exactly treated philosophically, but beneath the farce, the face-pulling and the sexual antics, something is being gently said about dreams and how they sometimes come true, and something else is being said about the western genre itself.

This should not be overstated; *Goin' South* is basically a romp. But it is a decidedly Nicholson romp, a Nicholson statement of some sort. Just as Clint Eastwood had great fun with his own image in his first film as director-star, *High Plains Drifter*, so Nicholson takes his own persona to the lunatic limit in *Goin' South*. Many critics accused him of 'going over the top', and the actor/director himself recognized that it was hard not to with a role like Moon and no one there to restrain him, but in a way the film works *because* he goes over the top, does create, in Derek Malcolm's perfect paraphrase, 'true grot'.

10

Overlooking America

*'It's impossible for words to describe what is necessary to
those who do not know what horror means.'*
Marlon Brando, as Kurtz, in *Apocalypse Now*

SEVERAL YEARS EARLIER, Nicholson had been wakened
at one in the morning by the phone ringing. 'This is
Stanley Kubrick,' said the voice at the other end. 'I
just saw *Easy Rider*, I was unaware of you before that,
and then right after I saw the movie I broke my leg.
Now I'm working on *Napoleon*, and my assumption is
that the prejudice of American audiences is that they
only want to see actors in classical stories with Eng-
lish accents. But now I've had ten days to think about
your performance and you have the one quality
which can't be acted as an actor. You cannot create

intelligence within a characterization for an actor. You have it tremendously, it's obvious, it permeates your work . . .'

Napoleon fell through but the reasoning remained, and when Kubrick required an 'intelligent' actor for *The Shining* he contacted the actor once more. Nicholson, true to form, jumped at this chance of working with one of the world's finest directors. He hadn't worked on a horror movie since Corman days, and in any case this new project was likely to be a cut or two above *The Terror*. If Kubrick's past record was anything to go by, they'd be more likely to spend two years on the movie than two weeks, and it was a fair bet that they wouldn't be using second-hand sets. Kubrick himself was intent on making 'the best horror movie ever'. It had to be 'plausible, use no cheap tricks, have no holes in the plot and no failure in motivation. It must be a scary horror story without insulting the intelligence of the audience.'

In the event it took more than a year to make, and most of that was spent shooting the interiors at Elstree Studios in north London. No one had any illusions as to why it all took so long; as Nicholson said: 'There are always insane and preposterous legends about people who work in movies and, because he's one of the outstanding people in his field, his [Kubrick's] legends are even more preposterous than anyone else's. The simple truth about Stanley is that he is the definition of how long it actually takes to make a movie. I mean everyone else is cutting corners . . .'

Nicholson played Jack Torrance, the film's central character and one of humanity's less satisfied members. He has no regular job, he's prone to excessive drinking, and he hides his sense of personal failure behind the proverbial 'desire to write'. To fulfil this

154

ambition he needs time, peace and the money to feed himself and his family. The job of caretaker in a mountain hotel during the winter off-season seems ideal. He applies for and gets it.

Accompanying him on this long vigil are wife Wendy (Shelley Duvall) and son Danny (Danny Lloyd). The former is the complacent-worrier type; she wants to believe in Jack's hopes for the future, but she's also anxious about his relationship with their son Danny. He's still somewhat traumatized by a beating received during one of daddy's more drunken moments. They all arrive at the Overlook Hotel as the staff is preparing to leave, and several dire warnings are uttered. Jack has already been told of a previous caretaker who axed his family to death in mid-winter, and now the black cook Halloran ('Scatman' Crothers) warns Danny against Room 237, where mysterious and dangerous events take place.

Left alone the family settles in. Danny uses the long corridors of the empty, echoing hotel as a Grand Prix circuit for his tricycle, faithfully followed by Kubrick's 'steadicam' machine. Jack starts writing, or at least appears to start writing, the Great American Novel at a desk in the cavernous lobby. Wendy services them both. Winter takes its grip.

Strange things begin to happen, first to the child. He has visions of two young girls – the axe-murderer's victims? – sees escalators exploding in blood, mutters 'Redrum' as if possessed by another voice, finds his ball being moved around by an unseen agency.

Jack's writing isn't going very well, and he begins visiting the hotel bar, where he has long conversations with (presumably) imaginary but highly substantial members of the staff. He'd sell his soul for a drink, he tells the barman, who duly fulfils his side of the bargain. Jack also goes into Room 237 after Danny says he's been assaulted by a strange woman – he has the bruises to prove it – and finds a woman in the bath. She's beautiful too, but when Jack embraces her she turns into a wizened crone in his arms. Or so it seems. Jack tells Wendy there was no one there, the boy must have bruised himself. She thinks Jack did it.

Most of this makes sense given two assumptions: Jack's going crazy and Danny's having premonitions of where that craziness is leading to. But from this point on even this reasoning begins to fail, because Wendy starts seeing things too. Either they're all going mad or something else is playing an important role.

She looks through Jack's now voluminous novel, only to discover that every page contains the same line – 'all work and no play makes Jack a dull boy' – repeated ad nauseam. The jig is decidedly up, and Wendy now realises – the audience has known for an hour or more – that a re-run of the axe murders is high on the list of probabilities. Fortunately though, this growing menace has created its own countervailing force, and Danny is now sufficiently psyched up to send, albeit inadvertently, a cry for help down the telepathic airwaves. Halloran, lying in bed in Florida, hears this 'shining' loud and clear. He sets out across the country by plane and then snowmobile.

Jack finds his axe but Wendy manages to lock him in the cold store. He gets out, no one knows how, and ambushes the arriving Halloran, but his family proves more elusive. Danny tricks his father in the maze by retracing his steps in the snow, and he and Wendy manage to escape in the providentially-supplied snowmobile. Jack is left sitting in the maze with his axe.

This brief description of the film's structure, style

and characterization-level helps to identify the reasons for the film's poor critical reception. In the genre's traditional terms, *The Shining* seemed an interesting failure. Horror films usually rely on three traits for their impact: characterization deep enough to elicit audience identification with the victims, story construction and pacing designed to create suspense, and sufficient realism to allow the suspension of audience disbelief. It is the viewers who are supposed to experience the horror, and they cannot do so without surrendering themselves to the situation of the characters.

In all these departments *The Shining* seems sadly lacking. The characters are insufficiently developed; they invite voyeurism rather than identification. To make matters worse, Nicholson's performance verges on *grand guignol*, more laughable than scary. The film is too slow, too deliberate, for any real tension to develop; all the events are signposted far in advance, and even then are rarely horrifying. From the moment the axe-murders are mentioned at the beginning of the film everyone knows what's going to happen. The only mysteries are the gaping holes in the plot. Who does move the kid's ball? How does Torrance get out of the cold-store? It's simply not real enough to be horrifying. *The Daily Telegraph* reviewer was far from a lone voice in thinking that 'the first requirement of a horror film is to horrify; it helps too if the story obeys some internal logic. *The Shining* does neither.'

So what's going on? Looking back ten years, it's interesting to discover that the criticisms levelled at *2001: A Space Odyssey* had been remarkably similar. There was no character development, the reviewers complained, the film was too long and too slow,

157

there was no tension, crucial developments like the computer's rebellion were left unexplained. And the end, well, who understood that without the help of the novel? It was almost as if all those factors, all the traditional components of a movie, didn't matter to Kubrick. He was after something else entirely. Clive James wrote that 'the orchestration of visual effects is far more important than the punishingly achieved and deservedly praised authenticity which distinguishes the film's individual properties.' The mechanics of the plot, the characters, were almost red herrings; they provided the necessary familiarity for drawing the audience into the mystery, but at the same time they lacked the depth necessary for a full audience identification. Or, to put it another way, they made it incumbent on the audience to make its own sense of what was happening.

The Shining can be approached in the same way, as P L Titterington showed in a long and perceptive *Sight and Sound* article. Kubrick uses genres purely as vehicles, and like Antonioni he uses actors only as images. *The Shining* is certainly a horror film, but it is concerned with real horror, with the state of our civilization, not the manufactured scariness which lesser writers and directors manipulate in their pursuit of a Hollywood lifestyle.

Its central characters are Torrance and the Overlook Hotel. The latter is clearly intended to represent America; there are simply too many relevant allusions for any other conclusion to be drawn. It is built on land once used as an Indian burial ground, close to the spot where a party of nineteenth century pioneers had been reduced to cannibalism. Both the hotel and the film are festooned with American motifs, Indian and contemporary. Wendy has braided hair, an Indian jacket, moccasin boots, a beaded belt; at one point she stalks through the hotel, past the Indian wall-hangings, knife in hand. Danny, for all his shiny technological toys and Mickey Mouse T-shirts, resorts to the old retracing-his-footsteps ploy when seeking to escape Jack in the frozen maze. American flags are glimpsed on several occasions and, most striking of all, an inordinate number of scenes are dominated by the colors red, white and blue.

Since the Overlook is a repository of America's past, continually preying on its present, it has to take an active role in the proceedings. America is not just the setting of the plot, it is a leading actor within it; the hotel releases Torrance from the cold store to achieve their common goal. The other characters are gutted; they have to be if they are to function as totems of the American present. Jack, Wendy and Danny represent the nuclear family as a paradigm of non-communication, and the different responses such a breakdown evokes. Wendy wants to pretend that everything's as it should be, and she's forever in search of minor emotional adjustments to take account of changing circumstances. Danny is Kubrick's hope for the future, the Overlook's nemesis, blessed with 'powers' which can help to undo the stranglehold of the past. His 'shining' is also, in Titterington's view, a metaphor for the cinema's potential as a breaker-down of human barriers.

Torrance though is the one who matters now. He fits into the family as the authoritarian father figure, he fits into the society as a primary example of its frustrated desire to create. His 'novel' adds the failure of written communication to the family's failure of oral communication. And, above all he's played by Nicholson, the 'intelligent' Nicholson.

It was essential that the Overlook/America should have a worthy, an 'intelligent' opponent. Nicholson plays Torrance and Torrance plays Nicholson, and Nicholson/Torrance is also Dupea and Buddusky and David Staebler. Through the seventies he's represented America's hope of finding a future amidst the wreckage of its age-old and recent dreams. When he breaks through the door with his axe, sticks his gargoyle countenance through the gap and mockingly gurgles the line – 'Heeerre's Johnny!' – which launched a thousand Johnny Carson shows, you know the game is up. As far as Kubrick is concerned it's all over. The sixties have buried the hopes of earlier times and now, as the seventies draw to a close, the hopes of the sixties have been consigned to a similar oblivion. Nothing remains but the encroaching cold and the thinnest of hopes implicit in Danny's 'shining'. And that is horrifying.

The trouble with *The Shining* all stemmed from the fact that Kubrick had tried to have his cake and eat it, to make both 'the greatest horror film' and a metaphysical masterpiece. He had, it's true, pulled off similar tricks in the past, but in this case the two levels work against each other; as Derek Malcolm perceptively observed: 'The genre within which the film is cast exerts too great a price.' Kubrick had made a film which, like *2001*, improved with each viewing, but in a genre which has traditionally relied for its impact on surprise and suspense, which can only be fully experienced on a first viewing. Kubrick buffs might get off on the visual and metaphysical imagery, but the majority of the cinema-going public don't take their seats with the director's auteur in mind. For most people a horror movie is supposed to be just that, horrifying at a gut level, not a multi-

levelled statement about life, the universe and everything.

The Shining might well be a classic film, and it certainly made a great deal of money, but the connection
between the two was almost purely coincidental. If
Kubrick is resolved not to spoon-feed his audience,
he should at least provide it with the occasional
spoon. Otherwise everyone will come away feeling
hungry.

11

ACTOR

'Wimsey said that everything had the defects of its qualities.'
Dorothy Sayers, *The Unpleasantness at the Bellona Club*

As THE SEVENTIES drew to a close, and as Nicholson edged into his forties, he showed no signs of a diminishing appetite for life. Through 1979–80 he continued to make movies back-to-back, and to cram everything he could into his fleeting periods of leisure. For Nicholson, one imagines, boredom was a disease which afflicted other people.

He found a lot to be depressed about in both the film business and the world at large. The trend towards 'blockbuster' movies he thought symptomatic of American culture as a whole; the search for profit, in

162

itself an innocent enough obsession, was becoming the be-all and end-all of movie-making. All 'they' were looking for was 'that one big picture', and such an approach was bound to 'narrow the avenues that are open for people to explore. It's certainly not good for me since I tend to shy away from those kind of movies.'

He conceded that cinema, like everything else in our civilized world, passed through cycles of fashion, and that even blockbusters occasionally possessed some saving graces. *Apocalypse Now* was one case in point. What was really worrying was that 'they' were doing 'a very subtle and insidious thing . . . they took the theatres and outlets away from the movie business in America, so they are now controlling the movie theatres by making very little product and giving the theatre owners very little choice. That is insidious because I don't think that movies can survive on the "event" picture forever.'

Nor did he particularly want them too. For much of the seventies the 'event' had been the level and explicitness of the violence on display, and this worried Nicholson almost as much as sex on the screen worried Mary Whitehouse. In an interview, he illustrated the point by recalling the story of an American serviceman in the Second World War who wrote to his mother that he couldn't talk to her anymore because his tongue had been cut out. 'Today,' the actor thought, people would say 'so what?'; 'in those wars torture was still horrifying, completely rejected by both sides . . . Torture in Vietnam has evolved to the point where they no longer torture the people, they torture the people's children in front of them. And these are the mass symptoms of escalating violence that come from a culture being psychically degraded through what it's exposed to. Working in films, you know, and I know that it's a very primitive eye that watches the film even in the most sophisticated person, and the more you're exposed to something the more you're inured to the psychic shock of it. That's what's happening on a mass level . . .'

But what could he do about it? Tell the world? He hated chat shows, had never appeared on one that wasn't exclusively devoted to films. He distrusted political activism, or at least thought himself ill-suited to it. He admitted to being a long-time Democrat, had got involved in campaigns for Robert Kennedy, McGovern, Jerry Brown and Gary Hart, but he was firmly convinced that the media decided elections in this day and age. If another McGovern came along, then he'd 'have to get in heavily and support him', but for the moment, with another actor of rather different persuasions asleep in the White House, politics didn't seem a very useful way of spending his time.

Making movies, that was a different matter. Over the years Nicholson had given his gold-plated backing to many a project in need of lift-off. He'd only taken the minimum rate for *The King of Marvin Gardens*, and there were other times he'd foregone the huge sums upfront which his pre-eminence justified. Usually he insisted on being paid 'from the first dollar that comes into the studio. That's the only way anyone involved in films should make a lot of money – by taking a certain risk.'

One of the most striking things about Nicholson is his thoughtful, no-nonsense, common sense. As a 'rebel' he's obviously pondered the contradictions, the apparent contradictions, in being rich and disaffected. He doesn't feel too guilty about it: 'In all honesty I feel like I could stand in front of a revolutionary court tomorrow, and if they did anything to me they would just be shooting people in masses. I am perfectly secure that I could face the most probing kind of: "Yeah, Jack, well what about this? Look at this couch? What about these paintings? . . ."'

He agrees that money leaves its scars, but reckons that people live on what they have regardless. In the mid-seventies, he says, he'd thought that with $200,000 'nobody could ever touch me again', but five years later he was carrying twice that amount in personal friends' bad debts. And it didn't really make that much difference: 'I wouldn't say I don't have a great life, but I wouldn't say that I didn't have a great life when I was working in a bar.'

The Treasury Department took most of it anyway, and unlike most Hollywood stars Nicholson felt no resentment. He liked the Federal Government, liked 'what they do with my money'. And he'd made 'a private oath to myself that I would never be active to institutionalize my position. In other words I'll never vote to protect wealth. And I'll never join the states rights group who are for cutting proportionate taxation.' If the revolutionary courts ever take him on it'll be an interesting case.

The perils of fame were something else he'd thought about, applied common sense to, and resolved to the extent that such matters can be resolved. 'It's not a burden as such,' he told Iain Johnstone. 'About all these things that are touchy, I think the job is not to have them be touchy . . . it's like, you asked about "do I believe in ghosts?", to me it's like outside what's naturally viewable. It's as big a waste of time disbelieving something as it is believing it. You irritate yourself if you think you're going to have privacy in a situation where obviously you're not going to. I mean I now have some devices to secure it.'

As for professional criticism, he tended to ignore it. Most of it, he felt, 'seems to be dealing with some

165

unreal world. It always seems to be saying: "Well, this would be great if Burt Lancaster or Hattie McDaniels was in it." But the fact of the matter is that Hattie McDaniels or whoever the hell it is was doing another picture and couldn't do this one. So you have to deal with the real world as it is.'

Of course, it's not so easy to be common-sensical in personal relationships, to let the intellect win splendid victories over the heart, and in the latter part of the seventies Nicholson experienced a few dramatic ups and downs in his private life. Anji went off with Ryan O'Neal at the beginning of 1976, and it was a hard blow to take: 'I did feel possessive. It was a bad time, but it was a time for me to understand other people's desire for freedom. While she was away I just floated. I didn't fool myself and say that it was very easy emotionally; it caused me a great deal of rage and there's no denying that.'

But he did keep his emotions 'in neutral', had relationships with other women, and refused to let wounded pride close the door to a reconciliation. When they were reunited early in 1977 there were no recriminations. 'We didn't discuss it at all.'

At the time of writing they're still together. Nicholson says he proposes marriage every so often, and 'sometimes she says "yes" and sometimes she says "no". But we never actually got around to getting married.'

Perhaps they both value their freedom too much. It's certainly not easy to think of Nicholson in a cuckold-role: his own well-publicized flings are too legion. Linda Kerridge, Rachel Ward, Princess Caroline of Monaco, Petula Clark's daughter Kathy, Margaret Trudeau and Diane Keaton are all said to have figured prominently in his affections over the last few years. But any suggestion that he's into casual sex is firmly rebutted. He's

166

interested in sex, 'preoccupied' with it, loves it, but he insists that 'you can feel the difference when you make love and there's love there, and when you make love and there's *not* love there. I'm not a Victorian but a fact's a fact.'

To those who consume gossip columns, it might seem that Nicholson did little more than make movies and actresses, but then gossip columns are not written for people with pure minds. In fact, Nicholson's life seems to revolve around friends as much as around sex, and some of them, like Rafelson, Beatty and Helen Kallianiotes have been around a long time. He has a love of good conversation – the TV has no place in his living room – and the walls of his home are covered with the paintings he has spent much of his wealth on.

At home he tends to cast aside the easy-goingness for which he's famous on-set. 'I tend to be very hard on the people around me. It is my serious problem and a pretty consistent one. I don't have a lot of patience with the shortcomings of people. My own, I think, are rather glamorous and cute. But the same thing in other people upsets me, and it's always the small things. The eggs not boiled for the correct number of minutes, for instance. Or the shirt the laundry has eaten alive. Or the orange juice not being fresh or Anji's stocking left on the floor. I don't know how to cure it. Like everyone else, I have tried to learn patience. I don't know how well I have done.'

He admits to being moody, something he used to deny because it didn't seem very romantic. Age and wisdom have made him less prone to such pretense, more ready to accept that people are like that. 'You can run the gamut of emotions all in one day,' he says philosophically, 'loving someone greatly in the morning and finding great fault with them at night. Even on the worst days you can laugh at something. On the day your mother dies, a monkey can make you laugh.'

He's not short on interests. Sport has been an abiding passion in his life and he shows it, to the point where his heartfelt performances watching his beloved Lakers basketball heroes are often as entertaining as the games themselves. He skis as often as possible, describing his own style, tongue-in-cheek, as 'massive poetry in motion'. He roller-skates at the rink run by Helen Kallianiotes, he plays tennis.

Like Bobby Dupea, this all-American sports fan shares a mind and a body with an intellectual; unlike Bobby Dupea, Nicholson seems quite happy with this arrangement. He reads – 'whole books, all the way through' as one dazzled Hollywooder noted – voraciously and widely, and he collects and enjoys art with all the passion he feels for the Lakers. When compared with other Hollywood stars – with most people, come to that – he's a real 'renaissance man', and it cannot be an accident that his film portrayals reflect complete, rounded characters with a conviction that few of his contemporaries can match. What other star, offered the role of Eugene O'Neill in *Reds*, would have gone through the playwright's complete works *and* enjoyed it.

He's quite clear about the link between his varied passions. Movies, sex, sports, literature, art – 'there's poetry in all those things. When I look at a painting I get involved. There is a moment of truth somewhere. And basketball: when you miss a play, it's a matter of microseconds. Little moments of truth . . . I was talking to Michelangelo Antonioni, and he had just done *Red Desert*, which is about technology encroaching on man. Antonioni was firmly on the side of nature, of a more natural existence. And every day while he was doing

168

that film, he drove to work along the Adriatic. On one side were the mountains, unspoiled, beautiful. The other side was encrusted with factories, all rust and corrosion. Antonioni said that he couldn't help it, he found himself looking at the factories rather than the mountains. Because that is where man was. Maybe that's how all those things tie together: they are the efforts of human beings to step out into the ether.'

*   *   *

James Cain's novel *The Postman Always Rings Twice* (1934) had been filmed several times, once by Hollywood in 1946 with Lana Turner and John Garfield in the leading roles. Now that the sexual passion which formed such a key component of the story could actually be put on the screen there was clearly an excellent case for a remake. Nicholson had toyed with the idea a decade before, mentally casting himself and his then-girlfriend Michelle Phillips as the star-crossed lovers. He felt then and now that 'this area is rarely explored in films, just making the sexual act real, and making it permeate the characters' behavior. The love scene has become kind of obligatory and yet nobody really knows how to do it anymore: you certainly can't track into the fireplace. And I'm not talking about pornography. I'm talking about modernizing sexual acting. You can have someone fully clothed moving from one chair to another and it's really charged.'

Sometime in 1978 he brought the idea to Bob Rafelson, who had just been fired from *Brubaker* for, allegedly, insisting on more control that the studio was prepared to give him. Rafelson had had a lot of trouble getting films made in the seventies; his integrity/intractability (depending on your point of view) was not

169

appreciated by the moneymen, and *Stay Hungry* was the only feature he'd managed to complete since *Marvin Gardens*. No doubt the idea of working with friend Nicholson once more appealed to him, and Cain's novel contained the sort of story which had always attracted him. It was about states of mind, not states of activity.

In preparing the script he and David Mamet stayed close to the book, at least insofar as the plot was concerned. Drifter Frank Chambers (Nicholson) arrives at the isolated Twin Oaks diner-cum-filling station, and decides to take the proffered job when he catches sight of proprietor Nick's gorgeous young wife Cora (Jessica Lange). Before too long the two of them are making passionate sex on the kitchen table, and soon after that they decide to run off together to the bright lights of distant Chicago. But they don't get far; after an argument in the town nearby she, and then he, returns to the diner.

Eventually she suggests murder, and he hesitantly agrees. The first attempt misfires, and Cora decides their dalliance must end, only to change her mind once more when Nick starts demanding children. Their next attempt succeeds, and they make victorious sex a few yards from the dead body. Then they're arrested for murder.

They get off because it suits an insurance company that they should, but mutual feelings of betrayal have temporarily cooled the relationship. She goes off to see her mother; he spends a few days with an itinerant lion-tameress (Anjelica Huston). Reunited, she tells him she's pregnant, and after several more untoward interruptions he proposes marriage. After the wedding service they are involved in a motor accident, and Cora is killed. Frank is left slumped over her dead body.

The plot might be a half-century old but the film is remarkably contemporary in tone. The two most significant departures from Cain's original concept lie in the characterization of Cora and the final denouement. She is no longer Cain's irresistible siren, merely an attractive young woman who meets someone as dissatisfied with life as she is. Their passion for each other seems almost coincidental. When she first suggests murder Frank replies, in a tone reverberating with seventies pragmatism, 'People get hanged for that, Cora.'

Since the twosome don't *seem* driven by the affair, they inevitably end up driven by the familiar plot, and the movie loses in tension what it has gained in atmosphere. Paulene Kael thought the direction 'over-controlled', and most of the film does seem over-relaxed, almost post-coital in tone. It's as if the characters never recover from the scene on the kitchen table.

Cain concluded his novel with Frank convicted, wrongly, for Cora's accidental death, but in Rafelson's film his punishment is purely internal, a seventies conclusion par excellence. The director seems to be trying to have it all ways, and ends up with a curious mish-mash of themes at cross-purposes with each other. The understated approach had succeeded in *Marvin Gardens* because the characters had psychological depth, but here they have none, and the down-playing of the passion which made the original Hollywood film work deprives the sequel of dramatic intensity. *The Postman Always Rings Twice*, Rafelson/Nicholson-style, ends up as an interesting, dispassionate look at passion.

*   *   *

Reds was built on a much grander scale, and so were its shortcomings, but for all the latter it was one of the most interesting Hollywood projects of the last decade.

171

The idea of cinematizing the adult life of John Reed — journalist, adventurer, political activist and witness to the Russian Revolution – had attracted Warren Beatty since the late sixties, for reasons that are fairly obvious. Reed was that rarity, a famous American socialist, the only citizen of Beatty's homeland to be buried in the Kremlin Wall; he was the key that unlocked America's hidden left-wing history.

It was equally obvious why no Hollywood studio had come within bargepole-length of dramatizing his exploits. As a communist he was ineligible for heroification. Someone was going to have to do some very smooth talking to get this picture made.

By the late seventies Beatty was in a very strong position. His last two films as a producer/star, *Shampoo* and *Heaven Can Wait*, had been both critical and commercial successes. Paramount took a deep breath and said yes to *Reds*. Presumably they gave Beatty a good idea of just how much they were prepared to accept; this had to be the love-story of Reed and Louise Bryant, set against a political background, not an agitprop tract with the odd sex scene.

Beatty, however, was not one to take the easy option, a fact which he made apparent by hiring Trevor Griffiths, the socialist British playwright, to do the script. Here the problems began. Perhaps Griffiths was unaware of the pressures being applied to Beatty, perhaps Beatty was only then becoming aware of them himself. Either way, Griffiths' first script proved too 'political', and he and Beatty spent three months in London's Dorchester Hotel preparing a second draft. This too was considered unfilmable, Griffiths backed out, and Elaine May and Robert Towne – neither of whom would be credited – were brought in to rearrange some of the sequences.

172

The filming was as protracted as the writing, with Beatty far exceeding his budget in an attempt to get everything absolutely right. The result was a sprawling epic that somehow manages to sustain interest despite its three-hour running-time and the lack of any 'epic' effects. The on-off relationship between Reed and Bryant, and her affair with Eugene O'Neill, takes up most of the first two hours, before the twosome find themselves watching the old order crumble in Russia. It's not history, but it is absorbing cinema.

The film's major fault, neatly summed up in the review-heading 'A Man, A Woman, and, oh yes, a Revolution', was its subsuming of political events, and Reed's historical significance, in the love story. It was also, perhaps, an inevitable fault. It was how Hollywood had always made its epics. As in *Gone With The Wind* or *Doctor Zhivago*, the audience was invited into the 'epicness' of it all via the love affair, which in turn acquired epic status from its epic setting.

The politics, when they do break through in *Reds* – and the film is less culpable on this score than most – are sadly inadequate to anyone with even a passing knowledge of the events chronicled. The dilemmas facing the Bolsheviks were not as clear-cut as the film pretends, though it could be argued that *any* knowledge of the period and country in question would be a step forward for American audiences brought up on red scares. But what *Reds* lacks above all is a sense of social tragedy; the whole thing is too personalized, it's almost as if the Russian Revolution occurred only to complicate the relationship between Reed and Bryant. Even *Doctor Zhivago*, for all its rampant Lara-theming, had this sense; there is no line in *Reds* which reverberates with the power of Zhivago's sad realization that the killing of the Tsar's family has been done to show that 'there's no going back'.

173

A further problem is Beatty himself. It's not that he acts badly, far from it. But he carries his own face into the part, he can't help doing so, and the Beatty the audience know from his life and other films is a survivor, an opportunist, a pragmatist, not at all the sort of man who'd risk his life for an ideal. He makes Reed into a contemporary American, and while the plot says he's an organizer, a skillful political manipulator, Beatty's face says he's the boyish anarchist who just loves taking a tilt at anything remotely tiltable.

Diane Keaton's performance poses the same problems when it comes to disbelief-suspension. She's perfect as the Louise Bryant the film means her to be, a woman perched between modernist independence and simpering possessiveness, but this too is a contemporary character, and it simply doesn't gel with either the real Louise Bryant or, more importantly, the film's supposed political thrust.

It's all too Hollywood: the big stars carrying their personae over from other performances, the felt need to structure the film around individual emotions, the consequent emasculation of political reality. And yet, at the same time, it's not Hollywood enough. *Because* Beatty is aware of the problems, *because* he didn't want to sell out on the political side, the central relationship is not given the traditional, heart-tugging prominence the tradition demands. We don't really care what happens to Reed and Bryant, anymore than we care what happens to Russia or American socialism.

On the positive side – and there is a great deal to admire in *Reds* – the minor performances are almost uniformly excellent. Gene Hackman jumps out of the screen in a small cameo as Beatty's editor, and Maureen Stapleton deservedly picked up an Oscar for her portrayal of Emma Goldman.

174

But it's Nicholson who steals the film with his superb performance as Eugene O'Neill. He found the man 'intoxicating', and it showed in his acting, prompting one reviewer to think it his best since *Easy Rider*, and another to comment that he 'sinks down into himself, and plays a quiet, deeply bitter man who makes each word count.' More than any other of his recent roles, this one showed just how fine an actor Nicholson had become, how convincing he could be in any one character-role, even carrying the burden of a star's face.

Beatty won and deserved immense credit for his production and direction. The latter, though hardly innovative in most respects, was notable for the use of real-life 'witnesses', whose reminiscences did go some way towards bolstering the sense of historical realism. The former was simply masterful: who, even five years earlier, would have believed that an American epic could be made around the lives of two communists? A small step for Beatty perhaps, but a giant step for Hollywood.

Last and by no means least, *Reds*, made at the toe-end of a cynical decade, offered a thoroughly positive view of love and politics. There *were* things, the film trumpeted, which were worth fighting for; there *were* challenges other than those confronting the special effects departments. The film's success may yet kindle a few idealistic fires.

Perhaps the last word should be left for Trevor Griffiths, who 'got some sense of the heat of Hollywood when you're making a movie, the incredible pressure, the extraordinary amount of dealing that has to be done.' He thought that 'to generate any kind of purity from that process is a triumph . . .'

★   ★   ★

The Border was a project not notable for purity-generation. Nicholson had a long-standing arrangement to do a film with director Tony Richardson, whose *The Charge of the Light Brigade* he'd much admired, and both men had a long-standing interest in the Mexican-American border problem as a movie subject. The story they eventually settled on was dreamed up by producer Charles Bronfman, and he enlisted Oscar nominee Deric Washburn (*The Deer Hunter*) to write the screenplay. Everyone seemed happy, and filming started the moment Nicholson was through with *Reds*, in the summer of 1980.

The film-makers seem to have started out with the best of intentions, not to say pretensions. All the Mexican parts were to be taken by bona fide Mexicans, even if parts of Mexico were to be played by Guatemala. Richardson and Nicholson were not the sort of men to make a *Borderline* (the Charles Bronson contemporary oater set in the same territory); both director and actor had a long history of making films with political teeth. And, indeed, some of the talk surrounding the project suggested that the line in question would be political, moral, you name it – perhaps this was to be the promised film about life, the universe and everything else.

It opens with an earthquake in Third World territory, terrifying to be sure, but hardly an explanation of why Mexicans are so desperate to invade the US. In fact, to judge from the lives of policeman Charlie (Nicholson) and his wife Marcie (Valerie Perrine), they'd be much happier staying where they are. She's God's gift to consumerism, and he's a totally convincing portrayal of someone thoroughly pissed off with wife, job and life in general. His idea of paradise is to go and live somewhere in the country, somewhere peaceful, but she's hungry for a duplex in El Paso, and persuades him to transfer to the Border Patrol. From this point on he's firmly caught between three fires: her ability to spend his wages faster than he earns them, his colleagues' desire to have him enter their corrupt world of Mex-smuggling, and his own desire to 'feel good about something', which eventually comes to focus on helping out the madonna-like Mexican whom he meets by the Rio Grande.

From this basic 'to corrupt or not to corrupt' scenario there evolves a considerable and largely incomprehensible amount of violent hokum. The original ending of the film had him wreck the Patrol HQ after discovering that his colleagues were murderers as well as smugglers. Suitably bleak. And too bleak for Universal, who vetoed it, demanding instead that Charlie should save the madonna's baby, and that the audience too should leave the theaters 'feeling good about something'.

This laughable denouement is enough to sink a film already barely afloat. Nicholson is convincing enough; he said he 'didn't want to appear like a successful film star but the poor sod I'm playing', and he manages it well. But poor sods don't suddenly turn into sharpshooters, ready and willing to take on their colleagues; only successful film stars do that. Nicholson admitted later that *The Border* was 'no more than an action melodrama', and so it is.

*   *   *

When *The Border* completed shooting in the last few weeks of 1981, Nicholson had been working almost non-stop for three years. There was no shortage of offers coming in, but he decided that he needed a rest. 'You become an actor,' he explained to Tim Cahill, 'because it isn't a nine-to-five job. You expect an

177

unscheduled existence. Then you become bankable, and you have all these projects spread out in front of you, and you know exactly what you'll be doing four years from now. Even the President of the United States doesn't know what he'll be doing four years from now. I want to get out of that cycle for a while.'

And he did, spending 1982 commuting between New York nightlife, the ski-slopes of Aspen and his personal spot near the team-benches on the Lakers' home floor. He deserved the rest. Since *Easy Rider* he had made nineteen films, and the list showed a remarkable diversity of genres, directors and roles. After the triumph of *Chinatown* he could have relaxed, played it safe, settled for dealing out morsels of the persona which proved so popular. But he didn't, he hasn't. Instead he has sought out new projects, more challenging roles, to extend that persona to its limits. In particular, his portrayal of Eugene O'Neill in *Reds* proved that stars could still be actors, and that Nicholson's own limits in this regard are next to non-existent. As Kubrick saw, his single defining quality as a star/actor is intelligence, and in an industry which forever tends to polarize the commercial and the intelligent he has an extraordinarily important role to play.

He wants a long career, and he's prepared – anxious even — to fertilize it with the mistakes that inevitably accompany the taking of risks. He says he's designed his career 'to be in the European model. Europeans tend to look more at an actor's body of work, and there will be peaks and valleys in that. Americans view art as an ever upward process. The next thing you do always has to be bigger and better. With a body of work behind you – good work – you can afford to take on a project that entertains you, one that challenges you, but which may not be bigger and better in the American sense.'

Terms of Endearment proved to be such a project. James L. Brooks, a director previously best known for his writing and producing of TV series like *Rhoda* and *Taxi*, had adapted Larry McMurtry's novel for the screen, and one of his major problems was finding a star old enough, big enough and self-effacing enough to take the supporting role of Garrett Breedlove, ex-astronaut in search of a new purpose in life. Nicholson, unlike most stars, has nothing against supporting roles—'I haven't done badly by them between *Easy Rider*, *Reds*, even *The Last Tycoon*' he said—and he couldn't help but be drawn to a first-time director who sarcastically asked some carping Paramount executives whether 'we're in danger of doing some original work.' Neither did $1 million to play the role dissuade Nicholson.

Shirley MacLaine and Debra Winger play the mother and daughter whose relationship dominates the film. In the novel the mother had many suitors, but in the movie these have been composited into Nicholson's Breedlove, and some of the best moments center around their coming to terms with mutual endearment. It is, Brooks insists, both a romantic comedy and something more than a romantic comedy. In his TV work, he said, he had learned '*not* to do anything for a laugh. Every once in a while I cut from this movie some very funny scenes because they undermined the reality of the piece.'

This setting of *Terms of Endearment* along the line between laughter and tears was one of Nicholson's reasons for participating. 'It's an edge movie' he said. 'It walks that very fine line. It's a comedy like *The Divine Comedy* or *The Human Comedy*. It's like Chaplin's movies during the Depression. I've done a lot of serious movies that I feel are successful because of the number of laughs that I've gotten out of them. Certainly *Cuckoo's Nest* is a great example of that.'

Nicholson also relished the role for what it wasn't.

179

After playing a psychopath, a sordid murderer and a border cop, he was 'looking for a slightly more redeeming social character.' More seriously perhaps, he was now in his 40s, 'and if I'm going to continue to grow as a person and an artist, I can't keep playing 35-year-old ideas of romance. This is a transition that I'm interested in making, and it's an area that I think has only been explored in sullen, lime-green tracts about the midlife crisis, or in a situation comedy. People have written great novels of this period of life, but this is probably one of the first really good films in this area.' The critics in America seem to have agreed with him. *Newsweek* thought that 'scene by wonderful scene *Terms of Endearment* may be the most satisfying Hollywood movie this year.'

Nicholson found it satisfying, too, on another level. In April 1984 he received the Academy Award for Best Supporting Actor for his performance in *Terms of Endearment*. Only Jack Lemmon and Robert De Niro before him had won Oscars in both the best actor and best supporting actor categories. Nicholson ended his acceptance speech in typical style, with "All you rock people down at the Roxy and up in the Rockies, rock on."

Other projects await him. On a personal level he would like more children: 'It is the one part of my life where I am not as happy as I might be.' When it comes to directing films, it seems unlikely that *Goin' South* will prove to be his last word. *Moontrap* is still unmade. Or perhaps he'll try his hand at remaking one of the Preston Sturges romantic comedies which he admires so much. As an actor he's said to be currently considering the role of Ernest Hemingway in an undisclosed story, and there remain several directors – Herzog, Coppola and Altman prominent among them – whom he both admires and has yet to work with. Further collaborations with friend Rafelson seem likely.

180

He's going to have his work cut out. He, and we, live in a world which takes books with beautiful titles like *Do Androids Dream of Electric Sheep?*, guts them of warmth, and turns them out as movies with names like *Blade Runner*. People will take him aside and say 'Forget it Jack, it's Hollywood.' But who would bet against him repeating his seventies success in the eighties?

Speaking of his future Nicholson says: 'I just hope tomorrow will be as good as today – and today is pretty good. I have been too lucky; I haven't had much on the down-side. Failure sinks in slowly and the feeling of success last for a day or so. What takes the time is the obligation to survive and most people don't have much time to see what is happening around them. That is the tragedy of mankind. They are not stupid: they just don't have the time to see what is right in front of their faces. And we don't even know there are splinters in the ladder until we start going down . . .'

A wise man, and a helluva good actor. Hollywood could do with a lot more like him.

FILMOGRAPHY

Cry Baby Killer (1958)

Director: Jus Addis. Screenplay: Leo Gordon, Melvin Levy, from Leo Gordon's story. Producers: David Kramarsky, David March. Co-stars: Harry Lauter, Carolyn Mitchell. Character: Jimmy.

Little Shop of Horrors (1960)

Director: Roger Corman. Screenplay: Charles B. Griffiths. Producer: Roger Corman. Stars: Jonathan Haze, Jackie Joseph, Mel Welles. Character: Wilbur Force.

Too Soon To Love (1960)

Director: Richard Rush. Screenplay: Lazlo Gorog, Richard Rush. Producer: Mark Lipsky. Stars: Jennifer West, Richard Evans, Warren Parker. Character: Buddy.

Studs Lonigan (1960)

Director: Irving Lerner. Screenplay: Philip Yordan, from James

T Farrell's 'Studs Lonigan' trilogy. Producer: Philip Yordan. Stars: Christopher Knight, Frank Gorshin, Venetia Stevenson, Carolyn Craig. Character: Weary Reilly.

The Wild Ride (1960)

Director: Harvey Berman. Screenplay: Ann Porter, Marion Rothman. Producer: Harvey Berman. Co-stars: Georgianna Carter, Robert Bean. Character: Johnny Varron.

The Broken Land (1962)

Director: John Bushelman. Screenplay: Edward Lakso. Producer: Leonard Schwartz. Co-stars: Kent Taylor, Diana Darrin, Jody McCrea, Robert Sampson. Character: Will Broicous.

The Raven (1963)

Director: Roger Corman. Screenplay: Richard Matheson, with a nod to Edgar Allan Poe's poem. Producer: Roger Corman. Stars: Vincent Price, Boris Karloff, Peter Lorre, Hazel Court. Character: Roxford Bedlo.

The Terror (1963)

Director: Roger Corman. Screenplay: Leo Gordon, Jack Hill. Producer: Roger Corman. Co-stars: Boris Karloff, Sandra Knight, Dorothy Neumann. Character: Andre Duvalier.

Thunder Island (1963)

Director: Jack Leewood. Screenplay: Jack Nicholson, Don Devlin. Producer: Jack Leewood. Stars: Gene Nelson, Fay Spain, Brian Kelly, Miriam Colon.

Ensign Pulver (1964)

Director: Joshua Logan. Screenplay: Joshua Logan, Peter Fei-
bleman, using characters from the Joshua Logan/Thomas Heg-
gen play *Mr Roberts*. Producer: Joshua Logan. Stars: Robert
Walker Jr, Burl Ives, Walter Matthau, Millie Perkins. Character: crew member.

Back Door to Hell (1964)

Director: Monte Hellman. Screenplay: Richard Guttman, John
Hackett. Producer: Fred Roos. Co-stars: Jimmie Rodgers, John
Hackett, Annabelle Huggins. Character: Burnett.

Flight to Fury (1966)

Director: Monte Hellman. Screenplay: Jack Nicholson, from a
story by Monte Hellman and Fred Roos. Producer: Fred Roos.
Co-stars: Dewey Martin, Fay Spain, Jacqueline Hellman. Character: Jay Wickham.

The Shooting (1966)

Director: Monte Hellman. Screenplay: Adrien Joyce. Producers: Monte Hellman, Jack Nicholson. Co-stars: Warren Oates,
Will Hutchins, Millie Perkins. Character: Billy Spear.

Ride in the Whirlwind (1966)

Director: Monte Hellman. Screenplay: Jack Nicholson. Producers: Monte Hellman, Jack Nicholson. Co-stars: Cameron
Mitchell, Millie Perkins, Tom Fuler. Character: Wes.

Hell's Angels On Wheels (1967)

Director: Richard Rush. Screenplay: R Wright Campbell. Producer: Joe Solomon. Co-stars: Adam Rourke, Sabrina Scharf. Character: Poet.

Rebel Rousers (1967)

Director: Martin B Cohen. Screenplay: Abe Polsky, Michael Kars, Martin B Cohen. Producer: Martin B Cohen. Co-stars: Cameron Mitchell, Bruce Dern, Diane Ladd, Dean Stanton. Character: 'Bunny'.

The St Valentine's Day Massacre (1967)

Director: Roger Corman. Screenplay: Howard Browne. Producer: Roger Corman. Stars: Jason Robards, George Segal, Ralph Meeker, Jean Hale. Character: getaway driver.

The Trip (1967)

Director: Roger Corman. Screenplay: Jack Nicholson. Producer: Roger Corman. Stars: Peter Fonda, Bruce Dern, Susan Strasberg, Dennis Hopper.

Psych-Out (1968)

Director: Richard Rush. Screenplay: E Hunter Willett, Betty Ulius, from the former's story. Producer: Dick Clark. Co-stars: Susan Strasberg, Dean Stockwell, Bruce Dern, Adam Rourke.

Head (1968)

Director: Bob Rafelson. Screenplay: Jack Nicholson, Bob Rafelson. Producers: Bob Rafelson, Jack Nicholson. Stars: Davy Jones, Micky Dolenz, Mike Nesmith, Peter Tork (The Monkees), Victor Mature, Annette Funicello. Character: himself.

Easy Rider (1969)

Director: Dennis Hopper. Screenplay: Peter Fonda, Dennis Hopper, Terry Southern. Producer: Peter Fonda. Co-stars: Peter Fonda, Dennis Hopper. Character: George Hanson.

On A Clear Day You Can See Forever (1970)

Director: Vincente Minnelli. Screenplay: Alan Jay Lerner, from his and Burton Lane's musical. Producer: Howard Koch. Stars: Barbra Streisand, Yves Montand, Bob Newhart. Character: Tad Pringle.

Five Easy Pieces (1970)

Director: Bob Rafelson. Screenplay: Adrien Joyce. Producers: Bob Rafelson, Richard Wechsler. Co-stars: Karen Black, Susan Anspach, Lois Smith. Character: Bobby Eroica Dupea.

Drive, He Said (1970)

Director: Jack Nicholson. Screenplay: Jack Nicholson, Jeremy Larner, from the latter's novel. Producers: Jack Nicholson, Steve Blauner. Stars: William Tepper, Michael Margotta, Karen Black, Bruce Dern, Robert Towne.

Carnal Knowledge (1971)

Director: Mike Nichols. Screenplay: Jules Feiffer. Producer: Mike Nichols. Co-stars: Art Garfunkel, Candice Bergen, Ann-Margret, Rita Moreno, Cynthia O'Neal, Carol Kane. Character: Jonathan.

A Safe Place (1971)

Director: Henry Jaglom. Screenplay: Henry Jaglom. Producer:

Bert Schneider. Co-stars: Tuesday Weld, Orson Welles, Philip Proctor. Character: Mitch.

The King of Marvin Gardens (1972)

Director: Bob Rafelson. Screenplay: Jacob Brackman, from his and Bob Rafelson's story. Producer: Bob Rafelson. Co-stars: Bruce Dern, Ellen Burstyn, Julia Anne Robinson. Character: David Staebler.

The Last Detail (1974)

Director: Hal Ashby. Screenplay: Robert Towne, from Darryl Ponicsan's novel. Producer: Gerald Ayres. Co-stars: Otis Young, Randy Quaid. Character: Billy 'Bad Ass' Buddusky.

Chinatown (1974)

Director: Roman Polanski. Screenplay: Robert Towne. Producer: Robert Evans. Co-stars: Faye Dunaway, John Huston, Perry Lopez. Character: J J Gittes.

The Passenger (Professione: Reporter) (1975)

Director: Michelangelo Antonioni. Screenplay: Mark Peploe, Peter Wollen, Michelangelo Antonioni. Producer: Carlo Ponti. Co-stars: Maria Schneider, Jenny Runacre, Ian Hendry. Character: David Locke.

Tommy (1975)

Director: Ken Russell. Screenplay: Ken Russell, from Peter Townshend's rock opera. Producers: Ken Russell, Robert Stigwood. Co-stars: Oliver Reed, Ann-Margret, Roger Daltrey, Keith Moon, Elton John, Eric Clapton. Character: the doctor.

The Fortune (1975)

Director: Mike Nichols. Screenplay: Adrien Joyce. Producer: Hank Moonjean. Co-stars: Warren Beatty, Stockard Channing. Character: Oscar.

One Flew Over The Cuckoo's Nest (1975)

Director: Milos Forman. Screenplay: Lawrence Hauben, Bo Goldman, from Ken Kesey's novel. Producers: Saul Zaentz, Michael Douglas. Co-stars: Louise Fletcher, William Redfield, Will Sampson. Character: McMurphy.

The Missouri Breaks (1976)

Director: Arthur Penn. Screenplay: Thomas McGuane. Producer: Robert Sherman. Co-stars: Marlon Brando, Kathleen Lloyd, Randy Quaid, Frederick Forrest, Harry Dean Stanton, John McLiam. Character: Tom Logan.

The Last Tycoon (1976)

Director: Elia Kazan. Screenplay: Harold Pinter, from F Scott Fitzgerald's novel. Producer: Sam Spiegel. Co-stars: Robert De Niro, Ingrid Boulting, Robert Mitchum, Jeanne Moreau, Tony Curtis, Donald Pleasence. Character: Brimmer.

Goin' South (1979)

Director: Jack Nicholson. Screenplay: John Herman Sharer, Al Ramus, Charles Shyer, Alan Mandel. Producers: Harold Gittes, Harold Schneider. Co-stars: Mary Steenburgen, Christopher Lloyd, John Belushi, Veronica Cartwright. Character: Henry Moon.

The Shining (1979)

Director: Stanley Kubrick. Screenplay: Stanley Kubrick, Diane Johnson, from Stephen King's novel. Producer: Stanley Kubrick. Co-stars: Shelley Duvall, Danny Lloyd, 'Scatman' Crothers. Character: Jack Torrance.

The Postman Always Rings Twice (1981)

Director: Bob Rafelson. Screenplay: David Mamet, from James M Cain's novel. Producers: Bob Rafelson, Charles Mulvehill. Co-stars: Jessica Lange, John Colicos. Character: Frank Chambers.

Reds (1981)

Director: Warren Beatty. Screenplay: Warren Beatty, Trevor Griffiths. Producer: Warren Beatty. Co-stars: Warren Beatty, Diane Keaton, Edward Herrman, Jerzy Kosinski, Paul Sorvino, Maureen Stapleton. Character: Eugene O'Neill.

The Border (1981)

Director: Tony Richardson. Screenplay: Deric Washburn, Walon Green, from the former's story. Producer: Edgar Bronfman. Co-stars: Valerie Perrine, Harvey Keitel, Warren Oates, Elpidia Carrillo. Character: Charlie.

Terms of Endearment (1983)

Director: James L. Brooks. Screenplay: James L. Brooks, based upon Larry McMurtry's novel. Producer: James L. Brooks. Co-stars: Shirley MacLaine, Debra Winger, Danny De Vito, John Lithgow. Character: Garrett Breedlove.

193

194